Peace and Quiet
and
Other Hazards

Peace and Quiet and Other Hazards

Ethel Barrett

FLEMING H. REVELL COMPANY

OLD TAPPAN, NEW JERSEY

Unless otherwise indicated, Scripture references in this volume are from the King James Version of the Bible.

Scripture identified KNOX is from the Holy Bible, translated by Ronald Knox, © 1944, 1948, 1950 by Sheed & Ward, Inc.

Scripture quotations identified LB are from The Living Bible, Copyright © 1971 by Tyndale House Publishers, Wheaton, Illinois 60187. All rights reserved.

Scripture quotations identified NEB are from The New English Bible. © The Delegates of the Oxford University Press and the Syndics of the Cambridge University Press 1961 and 1970. Reprinted by permission.

Scripture quotations identified PHILLIPS are from THE NEW TESTA-MENT IN MODERN ENGLISH (Revised Edition), translated by J. B. Phillips. © J. B. Phillips 1958, 1960, 1972. Used by permission of Macmillan Publishing Co., Inc.

Scripture quotations identified RSV are from the Revised Standard Version of the Bible, copyrighted 1946, 1952, © 1971 and 1973.

Excerpt from *My Utmost For His Highest,* by Oswald Chambers, used by permission of Dodd, Mead & Co.

Material from *Daniel* (Great Heroes of the Bible Series by Regal Books), by Ethel Barrett, © Copyright 1979 Gospel Light Publications, Glendale, Ca. 91209. Used by permission.

Library of Congress Cataloging in Publication Data

Barrett, Ethel.
   Peace and quiet and other hazards.
   1. Christian life—Anecdotes, facetiae, Satire, etc.
2. Barrett, Ethel. I. Title.
BV4501.2.B38412   248.4'0207   80-16036
ISBN 0-8007-1124-6

TO my sons and daughters-in-law, Gary and Marianne and Steve and Cindy. And to my grandchildren, Mike and Sean and Michelle and Tracy and Todd, who have kept my head in the clouds, my feet on the ground, and my sense of humor in good repair.

Contents

Peace and quiet—a thing devoutly to be wished. But a word of caution: Too much of it can sabotage our lives. We need a little clutter to keep our feet on the ground.

1

The Muscles in My Arms Are Hanging Down on the Wrong Side

I never thought very much about senior citizens, except for an obligatory nod, until I heard that voice. I was half-way across the room, headed for my bed, when it came crackling out of the radio.

"Is your stucco crumbling?" the announcer asked.

I slowed my pace.

"Is your paint peeling and cracking?" he went on relentlessly.

I stopped.

"Is your plaster chipping?"

I clicked my radio off at "chip." It was a commercial for a house-painting firm.

"Good grief," I muttered to myself. "For a minute I thought he was talking about me."

My bed was very inviting, the pillows plumped and propped, the bed desk loaded with books. (I have a nasty habit of keeping a half-dozen books going at one time; my attention span is short.) I sank gratefully against the pil-

11

Her hair was lathered with conditioner made of avocado and yo-gurt.

lows and reached for a book, but not before I caught a glimpse of the woman in the mirror across the room. Her face was scrubbed to a standstill, her hair was lathered with hair conditioner made of avocado and yogurt, and covered with a plastic bag, and though she was already plumped, she could have used a bit of propping.

Of course I'd had clues before: like that day I was picnicking on the beach with grandchildren numbers one, two, and three—Mike and Sean and Michelle.

"Give Grandmother the backrest," Sean said. "She's getting older."

"Grandmother's not getting old," said Mike.

I said nothing. I've learned not to talk when my grandchildren are talking. It interrupts their streams of thought, and you don't find out nearly as much about life in general or yourself in particular. So I just let the tape roll.

"Yes, she's getting old," Sean said again, seriously intent on arranging his beach towel. "Her face is old, her hands are old. . . ."

"She's not getting old!" Mike said, giving Sean a gelid stare that demanded silence. Mike should have quit while he was ahead, but he had not lived long enough to learn the delicate subtleties of good conversation. So, with the finesse of a goose, he plunged on. "Of course she has a few wrinkles," he conceded, "but that's not on account of being old." He smoothed out his towel. "It's just on account of *living so long.*"

I held my peace.

That was it; or so I thought. We hunted shells and did all the obligatory things one does on a beach, and I thought the subject had been forgotten. But later, back at my beach house, when I reached across the table to give one of them a yogurt stick, I realized the subject had been closed in my mind, but not in theirs.

"If Grandmother is not getting old," said Sean, "then how come the muscles in her arms are hanging down on the wrong side?"

The raspberry yogurt wobbled a bit, but I kept my poise.

Ah, yes, I'd had clues.

I looked again at the woman facing me in the mirror. I raised my arms. She raised hers. Indeed, it did look as if the muscles in her arms were hanging down on the wrong side.

The very next day, I joined a health club and worked out like mad—on machines and in the pool—to get myself back where I used to be. I could no longer just think about senior citizens.

I was one.

I also walked my dog, Hopie (whom my grandchildren had named, in hopes she'd be a better dog than the incorrigible one *they'd* had, who, after chewing up the contents of the house and yard, had mercifully dug under the fence and run away).

Anyhow, I walked Hopie on the beach, but in quite a different way. Before, I'd walked in the sand, with her trotting sedately alongside. But now I plunged into the surf thigh deep and walked fast against the pressure of the water, calling to Hopie to come in and do likewise. Of course she had the good sense not to do it, but I did it, not realizing that you just don't walk thigh deep without getting knocked over when the great seventh wave plows in.

Back home, I opened a can of dog food—the kind that has four cycles for different-age dogs. "Hopie," I said sadly, "we are both on Cycle Four. Henceforth, I shall call you Pokey." She wagged her tail. The phonetics were the same; she didn't know the difference.

I was too shaken to cook, so I went out to eat. The waitress cinched it, when she said, "Do you get the senior citizen's discount?"

Now all of this gave rise to a question. I had always stood up for older women when they came into a room. Whom should I stand up for now? Women over seventy? sixty? eighty? I couldn't decide. I'd start to rise, then hesitate, both my knees and thigh muscles protesting, until I'd wind up wobbling and quivering, halfway in between. So I decided to stand up for everybody, except kids; there I was on safe ground.

It dawned on me then that I was neither young nor old, but at the awkward age. But the awkward age, to me, had always meant adolescence—frantically seeking your identity—where you'd been, who you are, and what you're going to become. That didn't suit me at all. I knew who I was, and I sure enough knew where I'd been—I just wasn't sure what I was becoming. Actually, what I would become had never occurred to me before, and it was too late now. I was jelled.

Daughter-in-law number one had the right idea about old age, but of course she's only in her thirties, so naturally she was in a position to be a great deal smarter about these things than I was. She and my son and their children had moved from their beach house to a ranch in a very small town, where the sign on the general store said EIGHT HUNDRED AND SEVENTY RESIDENTS—TWO THOUSAND EIGHTY-SEVEN CRITTERS. They had to go to the post office for their mail, and a couple of weeks before Christmas, she noticed an older man coming in each day, inquiring at the desk for his mail, and walking back out, empty-handed.

One day, she really listened.

"No," the postmistress said.

"I was expecting a card from my son," he said.

"Look," she said, "this is Friday. If you haven't got a card today, you won't get one. We're closed tomorrow, and Sunday is Christmas."

The old man thanked her and walked out. My daughter-in-law followed him. She asked his name and told him hers, then said her family was having an old-fashioned family Christmas up at the ranch. Would he like to come? It turned out he would. After that, she found out he lived alone, was legally blind, and needed glasses, but had no way to get down to the city to get them. So she made an appointment for him, took him down to be examined,

16

filled out the necessary forms, and adopted him as a semi-official member of their family.

Now that's what you do, or are supposed to do, with *real* old people. But where does that leave the rest of us—or me? When do we realize we're senior citizens; for that matter, what *is* a senior citizen?

Age, like beauty, apparently is in the eye of the beholder.

I remember some gentleman once asking me how old I was. I told him thirty-nine, and he grinned at me peculiarly. I said, "What's wrong?"

He grinned again and said, "I think you are fudging a year."

I have never forgiven him. I expected him to say I looked thirty-five. The idea of looking forty was a catastrophe. In fact, forty was the most catastrophic year of my life. I thought life was over.

Then, a few years ago, I bought a home and had an extra porch built on it. Everything was great, except for the steps; they had put a set of temporary steps on it, to "tide me over." The problem was, they didn't come back to put the real steps in, and the temporary steps wobbled.

Each time Gary came to call on me, the temporary steps were still there.

One day, he decided he had wobbled up them for the last time.

"They haven't come to fix these steps *yet?*" he asked.

"No," I said. "I call them and call them, and they keep promising, but they never come."

"Well, what's their number?" he said. "I'll call them. And when I finish with them—they'll come."

I gave him the number and went happily to the kitchen, to make him a cup of coffee—until I heard his voice.

"These steps must be fixed by tomorrow," he said. "My poor mother is sixty years old—and overweight—and she's trying to hobble up and down those steps. She might break her hip or something."

I didn't hear any more. I was seeing blinding lights before my eyes. I finished making the coffee, waited until I heard him hang up, then walked into the den to tell him it was ready, trying to remember all the rules of graceful walking: head up, shoulders down, knees slightly bent, *derriere* tucked in, arms hanging loosely and swinging, ever so little. I did not quite accomplish all this. Actually, I ran into him—*thwack!*—like a bulldozer. "Coffee's ready," I muttered.

Back in the kitchen, I poured our coffee and we sat down. Now, I very seldom lose my temper—only on very rare occasions.

This was one.

"Why," I said, in as even a tone of voice as I could muster, "why did you tell him your mother is sixty? I am nowhere near sixty!"

He raised his cup toward his face in amazement. "Oh, I know you are not sixty yet—but I thought I'd get the steps done faster. . . ."

"That is not the point," I said evenly. "The point is, I am not yet sixty. And I am not yet wobbling."

There was a silence while we both stirred our coffee, although there was no need for stirring—we both drank it black. But we stirred and stirred, sparring.

We talked about cabbages and kings from there on out, and nothing more was said about my age. I thanked him, and he went home.

But he had given me a bit of a jolt.

Was age, indeed, in the eye of the beholder?

I thought of Dwight L. Moody, who when he was a stripling had said, "I'll think about God later, when I'm old—maybe thirty."

I thought of Moses, at the ripe old age of 120, ascending Mount Nebo; his eye was not dimmed, nor had any of his faculties failed when he climbed that mountain. He was going to miss his appointment in the Promised Land, but he was on his way to something far more to be desired; he had an appointment with God! I find it hard to believe that he dragged his feet. I think he scampered up that mountain with the surefootedness of a hind.

I thought of Joshua at Shechem, giving his "Let's take it from the top—one more time!" address to the Israelites. He reminded them of God's blessings and cursings. And his parting shot was ". . . choose you this day whom ye will serve . . . but as for me and my house, we will serve the Lord" (Joshua 24:15).

Now, I don't think he said that with a frail and reedy voice. I think he came on like a thunderclap and left the Israelites shivering in their sandals.

And he was 110.

I thought of Daniel, the night of Belshazzar's feast, when that fatuous and cocky king commanded that the gold and silver cups King Nebuchadnezzar had taken from the holy temple in Jerusalem be brought in and filled with wine and passed around, so that his guests could toast their gods. Their gods were made of silver and gold and wood, they had eyes that could not see and ears that could not hear and mouths that could not speak!

And I thought of that dreadful writing on the wall, written by a hand—no arm, no body—just a hand.

And I thought of their terror, when none of their magicians could interpret the writing; and how Daniel had been called in.

Daniel was an old, old man.

Do you think they dragged him in, holding him under his armpits? Do you think he was shaking and trembling, in his dotage?

Not so.

He strode up to the king, his silver mane and his silver beard flying in the breeze he created. I don't know whether he knew the proper walk: head up, shoulders down, knees slightly bent, *derriere* tucked in, arms hanging loosely and swinging, ever so little.

But I do feel that he was as robust and vigorous as he'd been when young, for Daniel had been addicted to two things for all of his life: health food and prayer.

And, as you well know, he gave the king the works, eyeball-to-eyeball (Daniel 5:26–28 RSV):

"MENE—God has numbered the days of your kingdom and has brought it to an end.

TEKEL—You have been weighed in the balances and found wanting.

PERES—Your kingdom is divided and given to the Medes and Persians."

When the befuddled king offered Daniel the gold chain and the scarlet robe of authority, Daniel refused. "Keep your gifts," he said, "or offer them to another."

Gifts? Daniel couldn't have cared less.

Not that he thought his life was over. He knew there was more derring-do ahead, and there was. For it was after that infamous banquet that King Darius was hoodwinked into casting Daniel into the lions' den—and Daniel came out unscathed.

He was in his nineties.

Then I thought of a woman I'd visited once. She was somewhere in her eighties and hideously deformed and crippled with arthritis. "But I'm young *inside,*" she smiled at me. "I'm just trapped in this old body."

And I thought of Marianne (daughter-in-law number one), singing "Jesus Loves You" to her desperately sick child. The child looked back at her mother with the wisdom of the ages in her eyes. It was as if she were saying, "I know He loves me, Mommy. I know Him better than you do; I've just come from Him." A few days later, the child was back with Him again; she'd lived less than a year.

But she had patched up an ailing marriage, brought her

grandparents' families closer together, and jolted her parents from lip service to total commitment—which influenced a neighborhood, which influenced a community, which spread to another community, which ultimately started a church!

Which is more than this senior citizen can say.

So the muscles on my arms are hanging down on the wrong side.

I'm still going to have to go some, to catch up with her.

2

Warning: This Verse May Be Hazardous to Your Health

> Wives, submit yourselves unto your
> own husbands, as unto the Lord.
> Ephesians 5:22

I have always been a bit confused about this verse. When I first saw it (though I had been a confessing Christian most of my life), I had been a born-again Christian for only a year. I had been reading the Word of God eagerly and applying great spiritual truths to my practical Christian living. I liked the inspiring portions the best, of course. The verses that got down to the nitty-gritty on practical Christian living, however, were sometimes hard to take.

This one was a stopper.

When I came across it, my husband was not a Christian yet. I was sure he would be, in time, if I put legs on my prayers and witnessed to him by my own Christian walk.

I had a naturally docile disposition at the time, so being sweet wasn't too much of a problem. And, from the cradle,

I had learned many devious ways to avoid being subservient.

My prayers and my strategy bore fruit, and in due time, as I knew he would, my husband became a Christian.

My first thought was joy.

My second thought was how to somehow hide that verse from him.

He became a Christian with a vengeance, however, having an avid appetite for reading the Bible. So I had no choice but to scheme how I could somehow explain that verse away whenever the subject came up, as I knew eventually it would.

In Lane Adams' marvelous book, *How Come It's Taking Me So Long to Get Better?* he tells how he once thrust his Bible under his wife's nose, showed her the verse, and said sternly, "What do you think this means?"

"Well, *sub*," she said slyly, "means 'under'—and *mit* means 'hand.' So I'd say it means *underhanded*."

He admitted that it had given him occasion to pause.

Inasmuch as I did not have Lane Adam's smart wife to coach me, I set about to resolve this thing myself. In the process, I made a number of discoveries about myself, most of which aren't worth mentioning at this point, except for this one: I was not as docile or as sweet as I'd thought. My real, very undocile, disposition had merely been in the pit stop, getting refueled, waiting to get back out on the track. This was going to take a bit of doing.

Of course my husband ultimately came across the verse, as I knew he would. And when he thrust it under my nose,

I had a sneaking suspicion that this might be even worse than I had feared. When we went to a Bible class and I raised my hand to ask a question and he slapped it back down on my lap and hissed at me in a stage whisper, "Be quiet; if you want to know anything, ask me when we get home"—I was sure of it.

Oh, well, I reasoned, I might not win the battle, but I could win a skirmish here and there.

So I dug in for a long stay.

But as the months went by, and the years, I had to admit reluctantly that I was not only not going to win the battle, I wasn't going to win a skirmish, either—not one. I'd have to settle for being docile and sweet at home and a tiger on the platform. All my aggression, anger, love, hate, bravery—yes, and fear—I could pour out of other character's mouths, as I told stories. I could hide behind every character trait in the book, and nobody would know that it was I.

Little did I realize that I was only on the threshold of learning what subservience really meant. I didn't see it coming; it sneaked up on me gradually.

My husband had an opportunity to go into partnership with a very spiritual gentleman in a small business. Inasmuch as he had not been particularly happy in previous jobs, he thought it would be a splendid idea to finally find something he really liked to do, and settle down.

I was tired of moving, so I thought it would be a splendid idea, too. I especially liked the fact that this prospective partner was so deeply spiritual. So we moved again and started to settle down, to what seemed like the beginning of a whole new life. I knew the partner was deeply spiritual, for he conversed in pious homilies. What I did not know was that he had some very strong opinions on this subservient-wife business.

This impressed and inspired my husband no end, and the two of them, aided and abetted by each other, set about to draw up a set of rules, to cover just exactly what was expected of a subservient wife. It didn't have a heading, but if it had, it would probably have been: BILL OF RIGHTS FOR DOMINANT HUSBANDS, or RULES FOR SUBSERVIENT WIVES.

When my husband ladled them out to me, he did so in pulpit tones, and sounded very much like he was reading. It went something like this:

1. I was never again to ask anyone, even a pastor or a Bible teacher, any question in my husband's presence. I was to wait until I got home and find out the answer from him.
2. I was to be in my husband's home at all times, and not leave it without his permission.
3. I was never to be allowed out at night alone (except for choir practice, in which case, I should come straight home at a decent hour).
4. I was never to question my husband's wisdom or decisions in any matter whatsoever.
5. I was to cease speaking publicly in the future; I was never to speak again on the platform.

Never to speak again? I pleaded my case earnestly with my husband on this point. I would cheerfully concur with all the other points—but never to speak again?

He and his partner were adamant on this point. I was never to speak again, and that was that.

Could I not honor the few speaking dates I already had?

They went into a closed-door conference on this one, and it was days before I got my answer.

Yes, they finally decided magnanimously, I could honor the speaking dates I already had—with this proviso: I was to be home, at all costs, in time to sleep under the protection of my husband's roof.

"But my date next Friday is in a church in Flushing. That's clear down to New York and on out to Long Island!" I cried. "And I was to spend the night with the Hutchins!" (The Hutchins were the pastor and his wife; I'd known them for years.)

The answer was still no. I had to be home, under my husband's roof. "But it will take me half the night to get home!" I persisted. This sent them into a closed-door conference again, and they came forth triumphant, with a detailed itinerary. After speaking, I would take such-and-such a train back to New York, and then a train up to our town, and from there I would get a cab home. There was no sense arguing about it (indeed, I had long since given up arguing about anything), so I reluctantly agreed. I would be docile about it, I decided—after all, when I got on the platform, I could be a tiger for one glorious hour.

Well, the great day came, and I went forth on my journey. When I got there, I explained to the pastor that I simply had to get home. I did not go into detail. I did not want them to know the plight I was in. It was so ridiculous, I knew they wouldn't believe it.

Immediately after the service, couriers were dispatched to whisk me hastily to my train, which would whisk me off to my connecting train, which would whisk me upstate to my cab, which would whisk me off to sleep under the protection of my husband's roof.

I told my couriers to just drop me off at the train station, and they did. That was my first mistake, for my train was late. When I got to Grand Central, I had missed my connecting train. There was nothing to do but wait an hour for the next one. By the time I arrived at the stop in my suburban town, it was 2:30 A.M.

The station was deserted.

There wasn't a cab in sight.

I stood there for a moment, nonplussed.

We had no phone at home.

Then I saw a policeman's car parked nearby. A policeman's car—glory be—a policeman's car! Did I dare ask him to take me home?

Before I could make up my mind, a policeman got out of the car and came over and asked me if I was waiting for someone. I explained my plight.

"Get in," he said. "I'll take you home."

I got in gratefully. *Aha*, I thought, *my husband was right. If I obeyed him (and his very spiritual partner), all would be well. I would see, in due time. I would learn.*

I should have witnessed to the nice policeman on the way home, but I must confess I was too upset to do so.

That was my second mistake.

When we pulled up in the dark alongside the house, I

fished in my purse, pulled out a dollar (a dollar was big, in those days), and slid it across the seat. I thanked him profusely. "I'm so grateful," I said. "Please take this. It's what a cab would have cost me. Without you, I would never have gotten home."

Whereupon, the nice policeman reached out, but not to take the dollar. It was to take my hand. He covered my hand with his own, got hold of my wrist, and pulled me, gently, experimentally, toward him.

I was nonplussed.

What did a subservient wife do now?

I disengaged my hand and repeated my profuse thanks. "No," I said, "I'm very grateful. Please take the money." I left the dollar on the seat and scrambled out of the car. He got the cue and went back to his previous jovial manner. "It's all right," he said. "Glad I could help you!"

And I went up the stairs to our apartment.

So the subservient wife explained to her dominant husband all that had come to pass. But behold, she withheld from him the information about the nice policeman.

That was her third mistake. Verily, she should have told all. For, content that their doings were right in the sight of the Lord, the dominant husband and very spiritual partner went piously on their way. They did proceed with their righteous doings, verily, with gusto. And behold, the subservient wife was the loser.

For it came to pass that shortly after that, the very spiritual partner began to drop in on the wife, and at odd hours

29

of the day, to pray with her about various and sundry matters. They would chat briefly about how well she was coming along, and then they would stand to pray. But behold, as they stood to pray, he would slip his arm around her shoulders, and then it came to pass that he would put his head next to hers, and then, verily, attempt to get them cheek to cheek.

Now she beheld that there was something very fishy about all of this, but she held all these things in her heart, wondering if she had not perchance fallen into a trap.

At any rate, the story of my struggle to get home on time sent them into another conference. All dates that had already been booked were promptly canceled. I was to speak no more, not under any conditions.

I was home now, but good, without any outlets for my creative energy. I could not even be a tiger on the platform.

I looked about me, in our cramped quarters, for some way to be creative. I read the last chapter of Proverbs over and over again. I could not spin or weave—but I could sew.

I bought remnants. I made myself clothing that I could never wear, except in the house. I made my husband sport shirts. I made him a bathrobe. I made him his pajamas. Then I made curtains and drapes. Then I made a bedspread. I tried my expertise at slipcovering. I didn't know a thing about slipcovering, but I bought a book and figured it out for myself. Before I was finished, I had everything in

I had baked stuff stacked to the ceiling.

the house slipcovered, except the electric mixer. Even the closets were filled with slipcovers—garment bags, shoe bags, purse bags—you simply could not get at anything without pawing through a slipcover.

After all this was done, I looked desperately about me for some other sort of release for my creative energy. I had already cooked everything that had ever been invented, so I turned my creative urge to baking. I baked chocolate eclairs; I made cream puffs; I baked cherry pies, berry pies, apple pies. I made a pie with everything in sight. There was not a food that you ever heard of that I could not turn into a pie. I had baked stuff stacked to the ceiling—with lopsided results. My husband could eat anything and still remain trim; I was slowly turning into a blimp.

Then one day, while I was waiting for a cherry pie to come out of the oven, I took four large kitchen matches out of the box and laid them down in a square on top of the stove. Then, with my mind on absolutely nothing but being a subservient wife, I took four more out and placed them on the first four. Then I took four more out and placed them on the second four. Then I took out four more. I kept placing them on top of one another until I had a nice little pile about two inches high. Then, impulsively, I took one match out, struck it, and lighted the bottom match. I watched as they kept igniting one another and shot up in a beautiful flame. When they had burned and cooled, I scraped them off with my hand and put them in the wastebasket. I thought that was the end of it.

But it wasn't.

As the days went by, I became more and more creative. I stacked the matches higher and higher; I built beautiful castles and towers and stood there and watched as my creations burned, curled, and toppled into a heap.

This would not be worth mentioning, if it had stopped there, but it did not. In subsequent days, I found myself sneaking out of the house to the store, to buy kitchen matches—boxes and boxes of them. I created towers and castles as high as I could, until they threatened to topple, then I lighted the bottom one and stood there fascinated while they burned. I had majored in psychology and psychiatry in my nurse's training and postgraduate work, and I should have known where I was headed.

I was praying and reading my Bible, but the needle had stuck on that one verse on subservience, taken out of context. The verses that followed had somehow been blotted out of my mind.

I knew a woman who used to tell her children stories at night and leave the hero about to be cast over a cliff or in some similar dreadful plight. She'd just leave the story there, her children trembling and wondering about the results. But the next night, she would always start her story cheerfully with, "But happily, he was not injured," and go on with the story, and somehow the kids swallowed it.

So it was with me: Happily, I was not injured.

The denouement was at hand.

We were invited over to the home of my husband's very spiritual partner and his wife, on one of our periodic bashes—which usually consisted of very pious conversation between the husbands. There was practically no conversation between the wives. I had run out of things to say, and she had not been known to say anything in years. In the two years I'd known her, I'm sure she must have said something, but I can't imagine what it could have been.

We were sitting around a table for refreshments. My husband's very spiritual partner was sitting next to me. Somewhere in between the gingerbread topped with whipped cream and the coffee, I felt his hand under the table, groping for mine. My hand was clenched under the table (I'd had a clenched-hand syndrome for many months), and he forced something into my hand—apparently a note. He forced my hand closed over it, and I held my peace.

The interminable evening finally ended, and when my husband and I got back out to our car and started off, I asked him to please turn on the interior lights. "I want to see something," I said, "and I want you to see it—whatever it is."

He pulled over to the side and we examined the "note." It wasn't a note at all.

It was a hundred-dollar bill. Neither of us knew what to make of it (nor do I to this day).

But behold, the very subservient wife told the very dominant husband on the rest of the way home about the "drop in" visits of his very spiritual partner, and how he had stood and prayed with her and attempted to draw her cheek to cheek. And behold, after they compared notes, it turned out that the very days he had dropped in for prayer, he had also sent the dominant husband of the subservient wife out on field trips somewhere where he'd be gone for all the day. And behold, they concluded that all this added up to some kind of hanky-panky.

The next day, in the mail, came another invitation for the subservient wife to speak. Should she turn it down? she asked her dominant husband.

"Take it," the dominant husband said weakly. "I'll have it out with my very spiritual partner this very day."

Which he did.

Whereupon the very spiritual partner dissolved the partnership and sent the dominant husband and his wife packing, saying unto them that he intended to ruin the subservient wife, if it was the last thing he did, for she had blown his cover and wounded him grievously. And verily, he set about to do this with all his heart. He wrote letters and made phone calls to every place where the subservient wife was likely to speak.

Fortunately for the subservient wife, the letters and phone calls were so venomous that the very spiritual partner lost his credibility and was hoist by his own petard.

Verily, Emerson was right when he said: "OVEREMPHASIS IS NO EMPHASIS AT ALL."

The pathetic part of all this is that it happened to three people who sincerely believed they were doing right.

If there is any lesson to be learned, it is this:

Behold, when thou findest a verse that seemeth to apply to thy practical Christian walk, verily, do not take it out of context. Read the whole chapter, or thou wilt find thyself up a tree.

No, I have not lighted a kitchen match from that day to this. I use those long, long matches now, and only to light the wood in my fireplace.

And if I have to have baked goods for guests, I buy them at the bakery.

3

How to Be Incredibly Awesome

I am an easy mark for self-improvement books.

I would never come out and admit this publicly, because I like to have people think I am very self-sufficient and don't mind improving. But I cannot pass up a magazine that features a new diet on the cover, or an article that promises to make me stronger or healthier or smarter in practically any area that isn't forbidden.

One that particularly caught my eye one day was an article on how to be awesome to other people. Now I knew I was not awesome; in fact, after my bout with my dominant husband and his very spiritual partner, I decided that I had a passive-aggressive personality. That's the kind where you remain sweet and pliable, while driving everyone else up the wall. You might be a pain in the neck, but you certainly are not awesome.

I had never thought about being awesome before; I had always been content to be merely mild mannered, kind, and lovable. But I was tired of being lovable; I was suddenly seized with a desire to be incredibly awesome.

The instructions were so simple, I wondered why I had never thought of them before: *Seek out only the key people.* If you can influence the key people, then you can influence the whole organization, group, or whoever you are trying to awe. There were other instructions in the article, but the idea of seeking out the key people was one that appealed to me the most.

But how does one cozy up to a key person? Does one just take the bull by the horns, as it were, and go right up to him or her and say, "Hello, key person, my name is Mrs. Barrett, and I'm seeking you out"? Or does one do it in more subtle ways—such as managing to be where they are and bumping into them by "accident"? But key people are always busy and preoccupied. The key person might step around me and keep right on walking.

My problem was two-fold, because I am a slow thinker and have a dreadful time making decisions. So before I had a chance to choose a strategy, let alone put it into action, the strangest *nonkey* people kept crossing my path.

Richard was one.

He did more than just cross my path; he dropped into it with such an impact that, like Henny Penny, I thought the sky was falling in. He came home with Gary and Steve (sons number one and two) after school, as he was left to his own devices until five o'clock, when his mother got home from work. He was very much the second-grader, yet somehow prodigiously old; he looked a bit like Win-

"Hello, key person. My name is Mrs. Barrett, and I'm seeking you out."

ston Churchill. He lived in a world of fantasy, complete with an imaginary grandfather, from whom all blessings flowed. This "grandfather" owned a ranch, a boat, a castle, a bank, and if Disneyland had existed then, he would have owned that, too.

Richard could leap into a recollection of one of his derring-do adventures at the drop of a hat. Most of them happened at some place his grandfather owned, and he always got the money to go there from his grandfather's bank.

He managed to put spice in the most mundane things. He'd spice up a bus ride home from vacation Bible school by hopping off the bus (after I'd paid the fare and before the driver got a chance to close the door), and we'd all scramble off, too, and chase him madly up an alley. He'd spice up a picnic by disappearing, not to return until just before I was about to call the police. I kept wishing I could find an excuse to ditch him, so I could get on with the business of awing key people, but the burden for Richard just wouldn't go away, so I kept "hanging in there" until I moved away to another city. I willed him to a woman who was, if nothing else, certainly awesome in prayer. Within less than a year, I got word that Richard—and his mother—and his father—were all being baptized the following Sunday. They'd been awed right into the kingdom of God.

As the years went by, it became increasingly apparent that I wasn't getting anywhere with my awing at home. *Maybe I would do better abroad,* I reasoned, so I went on a Mediterranean cruise to the Holy Land. Perhaps I could get some practice in being incredibly awesome with people who didn't know me very well.

But before I could find out who the key people were, Evelyn crossed my path.

I noticed her first, because she always seemed to be alone. She sat alone at meetings, she walked alone on the deck, she sat alone in the dining room—until all the other tables were filled and people reluctantly gravitated toward her table.

When the ship docked each morning and we got into our buses, she sat alone there, too.

I got on a bus one morning—looking for key people to awe—when I noticed her. There were plenty of empty seats on the bus, but impulsively I stopped by hers.

"May I sit with you?" I asked.

"Why?" she snapped back. "Nobody ever wants to sit with me. It's as if I had bad breath or something."

"Your breath is as sweet as the morning dew," I said cheerfully. "And I'd love to sit with you, if you want me." I plopped down beside her, before she had a chance to answer. "Isn't this all terrific?" I said.

She soon set me straight. It wasn't terrific at all; everything about it was wrong. The service was wrong, the timing was wrong, the program was wrong, the people were wrong, the leadership was wrong, *everything* was wrong—until I suspected that the Mediterranean Sea itself was wrong; the waters were too blue. And by the time we got to Jerusalem, everything there would be wrong, too.

I began to talk about the Lord. Surely there couldn't be anything wrong with Him.

She wasn't interested. She kept dragging us back to the cruise again, and what was wrong with it.

I switched the subject to her. Who was she? What did she do? Where did she come from? What was she interested in? Well, it turned out she was an executive secretary to an enormously important gentleman in New York. Her boss had suggested that she needed a change—a cruise, perhaps. So, being a Christian, she had chosen a Christian cruise. But all these crazy Christians were wrong, too, and she was bitterly disappointed.

When we got off the bus, I walked with her. When we stopped to eat, I sat with her. Whatever we did, I did it with her. And in talking with her, I discovered that she was an enormously intelligent woman. She could converse on any subject I might bring up, and she could converse on subjects I knew nothing about. I tried my best to keep her on these subjects, but to no avail. Invariably she would get back to what was wrong.

I knew by this time that she was a chronic complainer. *Well, at least somebody is happy,* I thought dismally—*the people back in her office.*

Each new day I swore that I would disentangle myself from her and get back to my key people.

And each day I found myself seeking her out, sitting beside her on the bus, walking beside her when we went sightseeing, and sitting with her in the ship's dining room when we got back in the evening.

It turned out that she not only didn't have a talent for joy—she also didn't have a camera.

"What?" I cried. "You didn't go on a cruise without a camera!"

"Why a camera?" she said gloomily. "What's to see?"

"Why, there are glorious things to see," I said. "You can't go back home without pictures."

"Why?"

"Why, to remind you of the wonderful things you have seen," I began, but my voice went off in a little tremolo before her icy stare. "Then I'll take pictures of you," I went on, "and send them to you."

"No, you won't," she snapped. "You'll forget all about me, once you are home."

"Aha!" I said with enthusiasm I did not feel. "Wait and see."

Well, I took pictures of her: on the boat, standing in front of the boat, standing beside the boat when it was docked, standing in front of the Sphinx, standing in front of the pyramids, standing near a camel (she refused to get on one of those filthy things; when they don't like you, they spit on you). By this time, I was sure that any camel worth his salt *would* spit on her, but I kept snapping away. Her in front of the Dome of the Rock. Her in front of Jesus' tomb. Surely that would melt her down.

It did not.

And so we went on.

Of course, by this time, the idea of being incredibly awesome to key people had been quite blown out of my mind. I kept on sitting with her, walking with her, talking with her—much to the relief of the other passengers. I had taken a great load off their minds. And she had put a great load on mine.

My spirits were lifted momentarily when she fell into my arms the last night of the cruise and thanked me for being so good to her during this terrible ordeal.

"Why did you do it?" she said.

"Evelyn," I said, "I love you. And God loves you, too. You must remember this. You must look to Him. You must not think about people making you unhappy. Your unhappiness is in your own mind."

It fell on deaf ears.

Well, we parted, and I went home and got the pictures developed. I sent her all the pictures that had her in them.

I got a prompt reply: "I didn't think you'd send them," she wrote. "I thought you would forget me the minute we parted. You really surprised me."

I read on eagerly, hoping that some kind of change had come over her thinking.

I was disappointed.

She went on thanking me at great length, but she concluded her letter with, "I went to my doctors, and they all agreed that my depression was furthered even more by that dreadful cruise and all of the things that went wrong."

Went wrong? I hadn't noticed that anything had gone wrong. It was a beautiful cruise for me, except that I had not been incredibly awesome to anybody.

Once home, however, I resolved not to abandon my original purpose. But my greatest deterrent continued to plague me: *Unkey* people kept crossing my path, such as that very discouraged Sunday-school teacher. She was about to give up, so I invited her to lunch and talked to her about the importance of teaching Sunday school. She was molding the lives of children who were the future church. Indeed, she was engaged in big business for the Lord. She got all fired up and decided to continue teaching, but I was no further ahead in my quest.

Then there was the lad, who after a week of conference, wanted to talk to me. I sat in my car and talked to him at great length. His complaints about his parents, especially about his father, were legion. I talked to him about authority and about love and about God—but mostly about himself. I said that you could bow down to authority and still keep your dignity, and all that sort of thing, and I prayed with him, for he really had a problem—an impossible father.

Then there was the incorrigible brat who lived next door to me, climbing up my trellis on my newly planted ivy, like an ape; in fact, I nicknamed him "the ape."

I couldn't stand him.

So what did I do? I invited him into my house to have some goodies.

He tore up my house.

I took him to Sunday school. He climbed up on the roof of the church. It took three men to get him down.

I took him to a program at the Christian school where my grandchildren went. This time, I hit pay dirt. He sat there absolutely *awestruck!*

Then his parents enrolled him.

When I went to pick up my grandchildren from that school, I picked Victor up, too. Then I began speaking in the school's chapel hour. I got so involved with the school, I forgot my key people and my strategy. I was forever picking up the kids when their mothers were involved in emergencies.

Then I noticed a change in Victor, *in his face.*

"Hey," he'd say as he sprang into the car, "I got an *A* in Bible. Do you know what I learned today?"

He quoted me Scripture by the yard, and I began to give him a dollar for every subject in which he got an *A.* I got so absolutely entwined in Victor, it was ridiculous. I could think of nothing else but Victor's progress. Then Victor got absolutely entwined with me. One day he ran up to me, wrapped himself around me, and said, "Can I call you Grandmother?"

Today, he reads all my books. He does book reports on them and gets *A*s. Is he my biggest fan? No; I am *his* biggest fan. I predict, at this writing, that Victor will be one of our next generation's great men of God.

I think it was about that time that I gave up my great quest for awesomeness. Apparently being awesome just wasn't for me. In all these years, the only one I had awed was Victor.

No, not even Victor!

He'd been awed by that Christian school!

I threw the book out. It was too exhausting, trying to be awesome. I'd settle for being just lovable.

But then I reread verses 4–7 of the thirteenth chapter of

First Corinthians, in the Living Bible, substituting the word *I for the word love:*

I am very patient and kind. . . . (Well, you are—up to a point.)

I am never jealous or envious. . . . (You've had a twinge, now and then.)

I am never boastful or proud. . . . (No, you drop into conversations the facts about where you've been and what you've done, because people are dying to hear about them.)

I am never haughty. . . . (Well, no—you have more devious means of asserting your importance.)

. . . or selfish. . . . (Not so you'd let anyone notice it.)

. . . or rude. . . . (Remember the lad at the checkout counter who put your package of liver upside down, so it leaked all over your cabbage? When you got out to your car, you had to make yourself go all the way back and apologize for what you said.)

I am not irritable or touchy. . . . (You're kidding. You're pretty good at hiding it, though; I'll give you credit for that.)

I do not hold grudges and will hardly even notice when others do me wrong. . . . (Then how come after you've "forgotten" the wrongs, they turn up in your dreams?)

I am never glad about injustice, but rejoice whenever truth wins out. . . . (I think I'll give you a passing grade here.)

If I love someone I will be loyal to him no matter what the cost. I will always believe in him, always expect the best of him, and always stand my ground in defending him. . . . (You'll be loyal, and you'll defend him—but he'd better not count on the other two.)

Good grief. In wanting to be awesome, I guess I set my sights too high; I'm not even lovable.

I'm still an easy mark for self-improvement books, though. And now that I think about it, the thirteenth chapter of First Corinthians is just about the best self-improvement chapter in the greatest Book I've ever read, anywhere.

4

Sometimes God Has to Lock You In

After my experience with Evelyn Foster on the Mediterranean cruise, I thanked God fervently that I was not a chronic complainer, as she was. In fact, I complained only on rare occasions and only when the matter was of utmost importance. So I thanked God that I had never been like that, and vowed I would never be.

So you can see right off that I was in trouble.

Whenever I have thanked God I was not like "that"— whatever "that" was— and have vowed I never would be, I have, within months, said it, or done it, or succumbed to it—whichever the case might be.

The case in point here is complaining.

It began insidiously. At first it did not seem like complaining at all—just discernment.

When I got back from the cruise, the first thing I discerned was that the preliminaries at the chapel were much longer than they had been when I left. They had always been unstructured, a fact that had once charmed me.

What a relief from the formal predictability of church services I'd been used to!

But it seemed to me now that they had gone from unstructured to chaotic.

The voluntary exhortations were great in number; the spontaneous testimonies ("Just a minute or two, please") invariably turned out to be monologues of alarming length.

"Well—um—I first learned about God when I was— um—No, I have to go back a little—before that, when my sister was married—I remember, because my sister got married in July and, by the way, I want you to pray for my sister, because she has backslidden. She started to backslide in October. I remember—I first noticed it then, and so pray for my sister. Well, anyhow, I first learned about God, really learned about Him, when my girl friend and some friends of hers—I first met my girl friend through another friend back in. . . ."

The music was structured. It was structured for a minimum of fifty songs, or whenever everybody was absolutely incapable of singing one more note—whichever came first.

That was when I'd start checking my watch.

The law of diminishing returns started operating after about twenty songs. First the tenors would drop out (tenors don't have much stamina), then the basso-relievo. The altos are of sturdy stock.

And, of course, the sopranos are indefatigable, so everyone would finally be singing soprano, but in tremolo now, trailing off in tired little trills that expired at the end of every line.

I discerned all this from my seat in the back row.

The message would last for forty-five minutes and was worth every second. My problem was that by the time the message got underway, I was beginning to worry about the unsung heroes in children's church, who were by now, I was certain, picking kids off the walls.

The solution to all of this, when it finally occurred to me, was so simple, I wondered why I hadn't thought of it sooner.

I would skip the preliminaries!

It might be wicked, but not as wicked as sitting through them in an attitude of increasing irritation.

I would stop at a seaside restaurant on the way to church and have my breakfast. I would keep my eye on my watch and arrive in church just in time for the message.

The idea, it turned out, was a jolly one, all the way through a delightful breakfast.

It was after that, that things began to slide downhill. I went to the rest room, and in there I checked my watch. All was on schedule. If my watch was working, I had ten minutes to get to church in time for the message.

My watch was working.

But the stall lock was not.

It was one of those little handles that you turn counter-clockwise to open the door.

I tried to turn it.

It wouldn't budge.

"Easy does it," I kept whispering to myself, as I cajoled it, eased it, slipped it as you slip a clutch. Easy, easy. . . .

51

"Easy *doesn't* it," I hissed five minutes later, as I jerked it, hit it, socked it up with uppercuts and socked it down with judo chops.

Why didn't somebody come *in?*

"Lord," I said ten minutes later, "I know this is a ridiculous place to be talking to You, but are You trying to tell me something?"

He answered me with Scripture: "Whither shall I go from thy . . . presence? . . . If I take the wings of the morning, and dwell in the uttermost parts of the sea; Even there shall thy hand lead me, and thy right hand shall hold me. If I say, Surely the darkness shall cover me; even the night shall be light about me. Yea, the darkness hideth not from thee . . ." (Psalms 139:7–12).

"But *here*, Lord? This isn't a bit funny. I'm humiliated."

"I have to go to great lengths to reach you, sometimes."

"Is this because I complained about the preliminaries?"

"I don't call it *preliminaries*. I call it *worship*. Anyhow, you complained, so I thought I'd give you something else to do."

"I'll never complain again," I said desperately.

"Yes, you will. You have a complaining spirit."

"Well, there are so many frustrated 'preachers' there. They can't make the simplest announcement without preaching a twenty-minute, three-point sermon."

"I have a hard time with that, Myself. But that is none of your affair. Let Me worry about it."

I sighed and checked my watch.

By this time, the interminable preliminaries, about

which I had been complaining, were over, and the sermon was well on its way.

The discourse was over, too, for at this point—glory be!—someone came into the rest room!

"You're not going to believe this," I called out, "but I'm locked in here. I've been trying to get out for at least a half hour."

"Can't you unlock the door?" a woman's voice came back. "Is the lock stuck?"

"No, I can't unlock the door," I said. "The lock is stuck."

Now, both the question and answer were pretty stupid. Naturally I couldn't get out, or I wouldn't have called to her. And naturally the lock was stuck, or I would have opened the door.

When one is in a tight bind, however, one does say stupid things, sometimes.

"Can you climb over the top?" she said.

"Too high."

"Can you crawl under the bottom?"

"Too low," I said. "When I get down on my hands and knees, I'm too high."

"If you lie down flat . . ." she began.

"I can't," I said. "The stall is too short for me to stretch out, unless I put my legs over into the next stall. I could do that, I suppose."

"You do that," she said, squatting down on the other side of the door, "and I'll pull you out."

"Well, I'm laid out flat," I said a minute later, "and now I can't move."

Between the breast stroke and the flutter kick, I managed to get back out.

"I'll help you," she said. "Put your arms out."

So I thrust my arms out as far as I could. She took me under the armpits, and between the breaststroke and the flutter kick, I managed to get back out of the stall.

I thanked her profusely and took my carping, critical self home.

"Move over, Evelyn Foster," I muttered sheepishly to myself.

Then the discourse came full-blown into my mind again.

"So," God seemed to be saying, "You get weary with the long preliminaries? Is there anything else you don't like about the way I'm running My church? Just let Me know. I can always find other ways to fill up your time."

"But I wasn't criticizing *You*," I said.

"You were criticizing My people," God said. "And remember, I'm still recruiting from the human race."

"But I wasn't *criticizing*," I persisted. "There's a difference between criticizing and using good judgment, and in my considered good judgment. . . ."

"*Judgment?*"

"Well, *opinion*, then," I said. "My considered *opinion*. . . ."

"I heard you the first time."

I drove the rest of the way in silence.

I know when to stop arguing with God.

Things have improved considerably since that time.

I was telling myself that very thing, only last Sunday.

The worship service seemed so spontaneous. The announced songs did not seem quite so many, and were interspersed with announcements and unplanned songs that just welled up from somewhere in the congregation and were picked up by everyone—sometimes hushed in wonder, sometimes swelling with such joy and praise that I thought of Isaiah, when he said, " . . . I saw the Lord! He was sitting on a lofty throne, and the Temple was filled with his glory. Hovering about him were mighty, six-winged seraphs. With two of their wings they covered their faces; with two others they covered their feet, and with two they flew. In a great antiphonal chorus they sang, 'Holy, holy, holy is the Lord of Hosts; the whole earth is filled with his glory.' Such singing it was! It shook the Temple to its foundations . . ." (Isaiah 6:1–4 LB).

I observed all this from my seat in the front row.

I cannot be sure if the service was actually shorter; I could not check it out with my watch.

I don't wear my watch to church anymore.

It's simply amazing, to find how much those chapel people have grown in the last few months.

5

How Long Is Your Gas Line?

The gas shortage hadn't gotten to me at all—or at least I did not think so. After all, I was working on a biography of Daniel, and my mind was far from the vicissitudes and vagaries of the gas supply.

The first sign that it was sneaking into my thinking was when I was describing Babylon. What a place *that* was!

Babylon! The biggest, the greatest, the most important city in Babylonia, if not in all the world!

It was a city about which you could *not* say, "You can't get there from here." For you could get to Babylon from anywhere. And you could get from anywhere to Babylon. Any caravan that was worth mentioning was either going *to* Babylon or coming *from* there.

When Daniel first saw the city, it seemed to shimmer in the distance across the desert sands like some daydreamer's fancy. It straddled the great Euphrates River, and was surrounded by a profusion of palm trees and a greenery such as Daniel had never seen before.

And the city walls! Daniel had never seen such walls! The outer walls rose 344 feet in the air! And thick! So wide were they, that they were made into a highway, with houses built along the edges. It was a place to take an afternoon ride and show off your late-model chariot.

There were four-horse chariots—large, heavy ones— real hay guzzlers, that could probably get no more than eight, ten miles to a bale of hay. Of course there were smaller chariots, the more economical models that used only one or two horses. A good horse trader could get you into one of those and you could get thirty, thirty-five miles to a bale. They were real hay savers. At any rate, there was no danger of sideswiping. It was wide enough for even the big hay guzzlers to pass easily.

So you could see that the gas shortage had seeped into my mind, even while I was writing a story about Daniel.

The second sign that it was sneaking into my thinking was when I emerged from my writing cocoon long enough to discover that we were into the odd-and-even-days plan. The only thing good about this news was that I was even, which saved me from all the derisive jokes about being odd. I'd been called odd most of my life; I did not want it to go officially on record.

This would be no problem, I thought. If I just got to the pumps before 6 A.M., I could take care of it in a trice and get back to work. I got up most mornings at 5:00, anyhow; this should be easy.

In theory, it sounded good. When I put it into practice, I was in for a jolt.

I got there at 5:45 A.M., to find a line of cars stretching for five blocks, clear over to the beach.

Empty cars.

Their owners had parked there the night before, locked their cars, and gone home. When the station opened, some of them came straggling back to their cars, some came jogging back, and some came back walking their dogs.

An hour later, when I got to the pump, I got my second jolt.

It was an odd day.

I was peevish for all the rest of it.

Next time I went, I took along a notebook and outlined chapters, made up titles, jotted down ideas, and wrote letters—whichever struck my fancy.

A week later, I phoned a friend on business. She wasn't there, so I left a message. "Sorry I was late getting into my office," she said when she phoned back. "I was in a gas line."

"Oh?" I said. "How long did you have to wait?"

"Well," she said, "I got through Esther."

"*Who* Esther?" I said. "Esther whom?"

"*Esther,*" she said, "in the Bible. And I started First Chronicles—got through one chapter."

I hung up, convicted. Why hadn't I thought of that?

The other day, when somebody asked me the same question, I said, "Psalms 139."

I'd been in line for an hour, without being able to get past that one psalm, and the hour had been like a moment.

There is absolutely no way, I guess, that time can really be wasted.

Unless, of course, you want it to be.

I got through Psalms 139.

6

What Would You Do If...?

One of the games we Christians play is the game of "What would you do if. . . ."

"What would you do if you knew you had only three minutes to live?"

"What would you say to another person if you knew you *both* had only a few minutes to live?"

Gary, who is a police sergeant and a medal-of-valor winner, is often interviewed, and just as often gets questions that are variations on this theme.

"If you were faced with an opponent, and there was no other way out, would you shoot him?"

One interviewer went so far as to say, "If you were faced with a man who was about to shoot you, and you knew he was a Christian brother, would you shoot him?"

There are many more; the questions are legion.

When we get these "What if you had only moments to live?" questions fired at us, especially in front of other people, we cast about in our minds frantically for a spiritual answer that will uplift others, uphold our integrity, and make us worth quoting. To dare to seem fearful or uncertain at this point would be tantamount to denouncing God Himself.

I have had such questions fired at me, and in full public view—on TV, on the platform, and in panel discussions. I knew that the questioner, and indeed anyone else listening, expected one of those pat and stereotyped Christian homilies that would make me look good and make everyone else comfortable. So I would spew forth one that impressed everyone no end, and stop them all in their tracks, for they then knew how spiritual I was. After all, your reflex reaction is indeed the most accurate barometer of your spiritual state. Mine was, you see, impeccable, for my great spirituality had rendered even the law of self-preservation inoperable.

One of my favorite answers was from personal experience.

I was at a conference in the San Bernardino Mountains. As I had spoken that morning and was speaking again that evening, I was in my cabin, taking a well-deserved siesta. I was midway through this very pleasant pastime when a jet plane came through a canyon between two snowcapped mountains and broke the sound barrier. Those were the days when sonic booms were rare, and you've never heard one, until you've heard it reverberating through canyons and ricocheting along the rocks.

I sat up in bed. Were the mountains tumbling down? Were they about to crash on me and squash me flat? Or, perchance, was the Lord Himself returning?

I leaped from my bed, and, clad only in my slip, dashed out of my cabin and ran a few feet, then came to a skidding stop, my arms outstretched, my head flung back—and shouted, *"Oh, God, how great Thou art!"*

If the mountains were about to crash down on me, I wanted the Lord to know where I was. And if the Lord had indeed returned, I wanted Him to know whose side I was on.

I had done this entirely without thinking; it had been pure reflex. When I realized it was merely a sonic boom, I crept sheepishly back to my cabin and vowed never to tell a soul.

But I did tell it, over and over again. So I remained impervious to intimidation on that question, "What if. . . ."—up until I ran for that plane.

I was hurrying to a speaking date and had misconnected with my next flight. The weather was very bad. But the people at the counter were on their toes and happily found me a plane on another airline going in the same direction. But it was a junky *little* plane.

The expediter was at hand, and, fleet of foot, he grabbed my suitcase and ran out a private door, gesturing me to follow him.

As I was running through the sleet toward the plane, a very strange thought struck me. *Nothing happens to a child*

*of God by chance. Nothing happens without His permis-
sion,* I thought. *Suppose—just suppose—that God had
made me misconnect with the big, safe plane and had put
me on this little junky plane because this little junky plane
was not going to weather the storm? Just suppose I had a
rendezvous with God?*

I was ecstatic! I raced toward the plane as if I were
rushing to meet a lover. I would see Him at last!

The expediter motioned me ahead of him up the steps,
and I clamored up, fleet of foot. He handed the flight at-
tendant my suitcase. I thanked him and rushed for a seat.

As I was buckling up my safety belt, it hit me like a
thunderclap: *I'm too young to die!* I cried in my soul. All
sorts of practical matters leaped into my mind: *I didn't
take out enough insurance. Whatever will become of my
sons?*

"Oh, Lord," I found myself promising desperately, "If
You'll let me off just this once, I promise I'll go home and
double my insurance and double my efforts to be a more
responsible person and a better Christian. Just leave me
around until they fly the coop and can take care of themselves."

That little incident brought me down several pegs. But
it took one more very embarrassing encounter to really
finish me off.

Once again, I was a speaker at a conference in California. I was sitting in the audience, listening to another
speaker; I was to speak the following hour.

I sat there listening with rapt attention, for the speaker was excellent, when suddenly my flow of thoughts came to a grinding halt.

There was a strange rumbling beneath my feet.

It felt like a vibrator at first, but then it grew in intensity. I realized I was no longer listening to the excellent speaker, because the excellent speaker had stopped speaking.

Earthquake!

A low murmur went through the audience, like a capricious wind going across a wheat field, and I realized that everyone else was feeling it, too. The murmuring died down into silence then, and we all waited for it to go away.

But it didn't.

The building began to tremble, and then shake. The lights above, which were suspended on long stems, began to sway like giant pendulums. Then the entire building gave a convulsive shudder and began to roll. I wish I could make it more dramatic and say they were great swells— that we plunged into the trough, then leaped up to the crests and plunged into the trough again—but I must be truthful. They were gentle swells.

It was at this point that the entire audience got up and made a beeline for the doorways.

In my twenty years as a sojourner in California, I had been trained that during an earthquake, one got away from glass and into a doorway or *under* something. Inasmuch as the entire length of the auditorium was enclosed in glass, there was no way to get away from glass, and the

I did what seemed most sensible—I dived under a chair.

doorways were already jammed with people trying to get out. The only thing left was to get under something. So I did what seemed to me the most sensible thing to do, at the time.

I dived under a chair.

Of course, in due time, all the rumbling and swaying subsided and finally stopped. Whereupon people came back in and we got on with the meeting.

I backed out from under my chair slowly, and not without difficulty (for I was stuck), reversing the tactics I'd used in getting out of the rest-room stall and hoping no one had seen me.

I sat through the rest of the meeting, listening half to the speaker and half to my pounding heart and feeling very, very foolish. For, in the next hour, I was to be the speaker. However was I to extricate myself from this colossal embarrassment?

I decided to tell the truth.

"Years ago, at a conference in the mountains," I began, and I told them about the sonic boom and how I dashed out of my cabin in my slip and cried out, *"Oh, God, how great Thou art!"*

They were profoundly impressed. I'd certainly had the right attitude.

But I plunged on in my confession, not because I was so spiritual, but because I was perfectly sure that at least *one* person must have seen me duck under that chair, and it was probably all over the campus by now.

I might as well out with it.

"So I dived under a chair," I confessed.

They looked back at me sadly, contemplating my lack of faith. Surely, as a speaker, I might have done something more spiritual than that.

"You see, my mind, like a computer, had just spewed out what had been programmed into it," I explained.

Silence. Sad, sad silence. I wasn't saying the right things.

"Well, I didn't learn anything more about earthquakes," I said solemnly, "but I did learn something about myself."

Silence. They waited for some spiritual application to come out of me. It did not.

"I need to lose some weight," I said. "For a moment, I was afraid I was going to have to go about for the rest of the week with a chair on my back."

They laughed out of all proportion to what was funny, as people will do in relief, after a scare.

We were off to a jolly start, and I plunged into my message.

During coffee break afterward, the conversation was, quite naturally, the earthquake.

"It was from Satan!" I heard from my left. "He did not want us to have this conference! He wanted to destroy it!"

"It was from God!" I heard on my right. "You see, He just waggles His finger, and the earth shakes! He wanted to show us His power!"

"I wish they would make up their minds," I heard from behind me. "Which is it?"

Jim Bakker summed it up best, when I told him about it on his "PTL Club" television program: "Well, one thing we *do* know," he said. "No matter *who* sent the earthquake, '. . . all things work together for good to them that love God, to them who are the called according to his purpose' " (Romans 8:28).

I wish I'd thought of that.

At any rate, I am now convinced that I have the right answer to the question, "What would you do if . . . ?" I faced it three times and came up with three entirely different reactions.

If you are ever asked it, don't flounder, don't panic, and don't try to come up with a spiritual homily.

There is only one answer, and it is simple: *"I don't know."*

And if your oh-so-spiritual questioner bears in on you, say, "I would never be so presumptuous as to predict what I would do under any given circumstances."

Stand on the Word of God. "So let the man who feels sure of his standing today be careful that he does not fall tomorrow" (1 Corinthians 10:12 PHILLIPS).

If your questioner is so dense that he still persists, say what Steve said one time, when he was still a baby. He was in his high chair, and we were all arguing about something, when he rapped his spoon on his high chair tray and bellowed, "Drop the suj-a-beck!"

His remark amazed us all—not because his counsel was so sage, but because we did not know he could talk.

7

Is What's-Her-Face Here?

Across the way from me is a house where a little boy periodically visits his grandparents. He never fails to come over to see me whenever I have my garage door open and am puttering around. We have long talks about everything and nothing; mostly, he talks and I listen. We've talked about God many times, in which case I talk and he doesn't listen, but interrupts with irrelevant remarks, indicating that I have definitely lost his attention.

Last week Sean (grandson number two) was visiting me, and the boy came over. This time he came directly to the back door and knocked on it. Obviously this was a matter of extreme importance. Sean answered the door.

"Is—ah—is—ah—what's-her-face here?" the boy said. "I want to show her my horny toad." Though I wasn't too flattered at being called "What's-Her-Face," I went out and inspected his treasure with the proper enthusiasm.

"It's a *horned* toad," I said. "One of the finest I've ever seen. He's a beauty."

"It's a horned *toad."* I said.

He left, satisfied, and for the rest of the day Sean and I chuckled about it.

"I can see that I made a profound impression on that kid," I lamented. "What's-Her-Face, indeed." But I got to thinking about the children who cross our paths and the profound influence we may have on their lives, quite unknowingly.

It put me in mind of a child, a little girl (and this is a true story) who visited her aunt's farm for an entire summer and who blundered into the life of a lady up the road. She was not seeking the lady out; indeed, she did not know the lady existed. She merely ventured up the road on an aimless walk, looking for wild flowers. The landscape was parched, baking in the sun. The Queen Anne's lace and the goldenrod and the Indian paintbrush were colorless and dusty, coated with the dirt insolently thrown at them by the tractors and wagons that rumbled by.

But when she wandered into the lady's front yard, it was like stepping into another world. The lawn was a lush, green carpet, kept cool under the giant branches of ancient oaks. The garden that bordered it was a riot of color—snapdragons, nasturtiums, bluebells, and every kind of daisy, with hollyhocks towering by the fence in the rear. Into that picture-book setting, some white leghorn hens strutted, pecking and clucking, busy about their own affairs, oblivious to the child.

"They've found a way to get out of the coop again," a voice said, and the child looked up, startled when she realized she was not alone. There on the porch stood the most

75

beautiful lady the child had ever seen. Actually, she was very prim and ordinary looking, but to the child, she seemed like a glamorous fairy godmother. Minutes later, they were sitting on the low porch that took up the entire side of the sprawling, white house. The child fell under the spell of the lady's easy conversation, until she quite forgot her shyness and was soon chattering on her own, as she had never done with strangers before.

The casual afternoon grew into a working relationship, for the lady gave the child a penny for every twenty white chicken feathers she gathered from the lawn. After that ritual was taken care of, they would sit on the porch and talk about whatever came their way—flowers and poems and clothes and stories and hopes and the sheer gossamer beauty of spiderwebs and whatever interested little girls.

They talked about God—not much, but they did talk about Him—not in personal terms, but with great awe and respect. And they knew and appreciated profoundly that it was He who sent the rain and decreed the way that calves and kittens were born. On rainy days, they went inside, and the child pumped an antique organ and sang tuneless ditties that she fancied were pleasing to the lady's ears.

When the first sign of autumn came, the lady showed the child how to collect seeds from the flowers, and they talked of God again. Then they sat on the porch, breathless before the blazing landscape, and remarked solemnly how extravagant God was that autumn. When it was time for the child to leave for her city home, they promised they would get together again.

But, of course, such sheer enchantment and intense joy could never really be repeated. The child came back to her aunt's farm periodically for shorter visits, but she had other interests now. Except for dropping by once in a while for a perfunctory chat, she was too busy to care about chicken feathers or long talks or stories or pumping the antique organ.

Then the serious business of getting ready for life crowded in. First there was high school, then three years of nursing school, then a year's postgraduate course, and the child was now a young woman, encompassed with the veneer of adulthood. Her childish dreams were buried forever with her talks about God, and she became a hardheaded, pragmatic, no-nonsense registered nurse. She traveled widely, living to excess, and saw to it that her veneer stayed intact and unpenetrable.

Then one day she happened upon a private-duty case in which, except for an hour or two in the morning, her patient did not need or want her ministrations. So she took to walking around the hospital and through the charity wards, chatting with patients, doing little errands for them, and in general occupying herself until visiting hours were over and it was time for her to go back to her duties. That's how it happened that she stepped into a room and had the strange sensation that she had stepped into another world.

It was while she was walking past an open door on the charity floor that she heard someone moaning in the room. She went in, to see if there was anything she could do. The patient was so old and cadaverous that she could not tell whether it was a man or a woman. It was a woman, with her hair drawn up to the top of her head and tied securely with a bandage, to keep it out of her face. Her wrists were tied with bandages to the head of the bed, and the crib sides of the bed were up. The woman was toothless, her eyes sunken in, and she was moaning and muttering incoherently, as if in great anguish and trying to make someone hear. The nurse untied her wrists and rubbed them and smoothed stray locks of hair upward, crooning perfunctory words of comfort that had no meaning, for her heart was not in it.

And then she had a sudden flash of insight, such as she had never experienced before. It astonished her, it was so strong and compelling. She went to the foot of the bed, where the steel-covered charts were slung over a rod that was there for that purpose, back in those days. She opened the chart and looked at the name. Then she knew what she had already known, when she had first seen the woman.

It was the beautiful lady of her childhood.

The nurse realized in a flash that she had been older, really, than the child had realized and not fairy-godmother beautiful at all. All her beauty had been in the child's eyes. The nurse put the chart back on the rack and went again to the side of the bed. This time she hiked herself upon it and put her hands under the old woman's shoulders and drew her up to her breast, and began to rock her back and forth, as if she were a child.

"Don't you remember me?" she asked. "I'm the child

who picked up your chicken feathers and took home bouquets from your garden. We sat and talked on your porch. Don't you remember?"

The old woman moaned, and her hands groped in the air. The nurse took hold of one of her wrists with her free hand and kissed it, and her tears dropped on it.

"I loved you so," she said. "I loved you so. It's me—it's me—it's me. And God loves you, too. You remember?" In between rocking the woman and crooning to her, she periodically raised her face and said, "Oh, God, make her hear me. Make her hear me." Incredibly, the old woman stopped moaning. The nurse held her until her arms ached, and then gently let her down and retied the wrists and put the crib side back up and went to her duties.

She would go back the next day, the first chance she got, the nurse thought. She would rock the old woman again and comfort her and coax her out of her coma.

But the next day, when she looked in the room, it was empty and scrubbed, ready for the next patient; the old woman was gone. The nurse inquired about her at the nurses' station down the hall. She had died in the night. No, she had had no visitors. She had no family. She was a charity case; no one knew where they had taken her.

So the nurse went on to her duties, but not before she went back and stood for a moment in the bare, impersonal room where the old woman had been.

I never thanked her, she thought. *I never thanked her, as a child. I never let her know how much, how very much, she meant to me—that for one glorious summer, she was the very center of my existence.*

The name of the child—and the name of the nurse—was, as you've probably guessed, Ethel Barrett.

It came to me then, as I stood in that empty hospital room—the hardheaded, pragmatic, no-nonsense registered nurse—that with the thoughtlessness of children, I had drunk in all she could give, with no capacity to be grateful. I thought of how I had inadvertently stumbled into her life and how profoundly she had affected me, and how I'd forgotten our talks about flowers and dreams and the gossamer beauty of spiderwebs—and about God. I cannot be sure, but that summer might have borne the seed for my first real, earnest search for God.

I'm thinking now of the boy who knocked on my door and said, "Is—ah—What's-Her-Face here? I want to show her my horny toad."

I'm thinking of all the children who bungle across my path. What are they really searching for, not knowing? Why has God brought them to me? Why don't I listen to what's beyond what they're saying?

The next time that horny-toad kid crosses my path, I'm going to invite him into my house.

And sit him down.

And talk to him about Jesus.

8

The Pygmalion Syndrome

It has been said that our personalities can be changed by
our grooming and the clothing we wear. Many a caterpil-
lar has looked up at a butterfly soaring overhead and said,
"You'll never catch *me* up in one of those things" and later
eaten his words. And many a person has also enjoyed a
metamorphosis, given a change of raiment and circumstances.

It's the old Pygmalion story, and it goes back to ancient
mythology. Pygmalion was the king of Cyprus, but he was
also a sculptor. He sculpted an ivory statue of a maiden
that was so beautiful he fell in love with it. As the story
goes, Pygmalion prayed to Aphrodite, and in response to
his prayers, the statue was brought to life.

The myth of Pygmalion was brought to life much later
by George Bernard Shaw in 1912. It was again brought to
life in living color by *My Fair Lady* in the 1950s.

The story was essentially the same. A wealthy and
learned gentleman picked up a waif from the streets, sim-

ply to prove the theory that our personalities can be changed by our grooming and appearance. He took the waif into his home and had her educated and polished to a fare-thee-well, adorned her with the most exquisite clothes and jewelry, and lo, she *did* "come alive." Not only her appearance, but her whole personality, underwent a metamorphosis. Ultimately, he married her.

Though this principle is not infallible, I suspect there is some truth in it, for I have seen it happen over and over again. I could cite you many examples of changes wrought by grooming and apparel, but the most striking one (in more ways than one, as you shall see), concerns Steve (son number two), when he was doing his fifth stint abroad for the army, this time in Korea.

He was in charge of a counterintelligence field office, and his interpreter was a charming Korean man named Mr. Kim. I knew about Mr. Kim. Steve had written me about him. Even by Korean standards, he was a small man—five foot four, 132 pounds—with delicate porcelain features and coke-bottle-thick glasses. He was mild mannered and very, very humble.

Steve, on the other hand, was a much bigger man, very macho, and very husky. Well, *husky* isn't actually what he was. His wife came right out and told him what he was— paunchy—fifty pounds paunchy.

While he was in Korea, he decided to do something about changing his image and profile. He would school himself in one of the martial arts. In Korea, the national martial art was Taekwondo (pronounced tay-kwan-doe) which is a devastatingly effective form of karate.

But I'll let Steve take it from here, in his own words:

Dear Mom:

Nothing much to report from here right now, except I got started on my martial-arts program. I called Kim in to my office the other day and asked him if he was familiar with Taekwondo.

"Ah yes," he said, bowing and nodding. "Excellent exercise and general physical conditioning, but it requires much strict discipline."

"I'd like to take it up," I said. "Can you recommend an instructor?"

"Mr. Barrett," he said "I hold a fifth-degree black belt in Taekwondo. And I would be most honored if you would allow me to teach you."

I told him great, and that naturally I'd pay the going rate. But he protested emphatically. "Oh *no*," he kept saying, "I would never take pay for such an honor." There was no way I could talk him out of it, so we made a date to meet at the gym that evening; Kim would bring a *Tobuk* for me.

So that night we met, and the mild-mannered, self-effacing Mr. Kim bowed, gave me my *Tobuk*, and pointed to a room where I could change. I did, and then went to the room reserved for the martial arts and waited for my first lesson in Taekwondo.

Wham! The door flew open, and the man who a mo-

Mild-mannered Clark Kent burst into the room like Superman.

ment before had been mild-mannered Clark Kent, came bursting into the room like Superman. I hardly recognized him. The coke-bottle glasses were gone, his chest was puffed out, his jaw was set, and his eyes were as cold as a hungry shark's. Actually he's thirty-seven, but he looked like twenty-five. He thrust an armload of protective padding at me and said, "Put these on."

As I did, my mind was racing madly, trying to formulate my strategy: *Stay calm, pace yourself, don't get angry, don't hit him too hard—after all, the lessons are free.*

We squared off in the middle of the floor and I was mentally prepared to disassemble this little wimp, if he tried to play too rough.

"Try to hit me, Mr. Barrett," he said quietly, "and give it—how do you say?—your best shot."

I moved in cautiously, saw an opening, and let loose with a killing barrage of kicks and punches—but Kim wasn't there. I spun around, and he gave me three solid kicks to the side of my head before I could get my hands up.

Mom, I pulled out all the stops. I threw all caution aside. I charged like a rabid dog. I punched, I kicked, I flailed. But I never touched Mr. Kim. He was on me like a grass burr. For every punch I threw, he would give two or three bone-jarring shots to my tender, pink body. Finally, and I'd like to think out of a feeling of compassion, he ended the match like a mongoose dispatches the cobra when he tires of the game. With a flurry of kicks, he sent me flying through the air like a duffel bag, and I landed on my brain in the corner. I lay there wheezing, tasting the blood in my mouth, and nursing what were later diagnosed as four broken ribs.

Mr. Kim walked over to me and squatted down. The little Philistine wasn't even breathing hard! He spoke very quietly. "Mr. Barrett, you must not be angry with me, for I have given you three invaluable lessons: A man's size and appearance have nothing to do with his fighting ability; to become proficient in the art will require discipline such as you've never known before. And, in the office, you are the unquestioned master."

"Yes," I wheezed. "I read you."

"But in the gym," he went on, *"I am king."*

Convinced that I had spent the last thirty minutes in a Waring blender, I re-evaluated my opinion of Mr. Kim. At 132 pounds, he was the biggest man I'd ever met.

Take care of yourself, Mom, and for pity's sake, don't take up Taekwondo. I'm going to continue, soon's my ribs heal; I'm going to get at least a black belt, if it kills me.

Love,
Son #2

I learned later that Mr. Kim was as good as his word. Back in the office, he reverted to being mild mannered and self-effacing again. But I do suspect that behind those coke-bottle glasses there might have been a twinkle, for in that *Tobuk, in that black belt,* he was invincible.

Though it isn't true of all of us, some of us are intimidated by clothes, and most of us are, if not intimidated, affected by them, one way or the other. I like to think that, if ever grave misfortune befell me—yes, even the horror of a concentration camp—God would give me the grace to stand tall in dignity, as a child of the King, even in the meanest clothing—knowing that there is a change of clothing that is permanent, and that is the garment of righteousness.

In my book *Chronicles of Mansoul,* Conscience and Will and Understanding go out of the gates of Mansoul to meet Prince Emmanuel and ask his forgiveness.

"Have you nothing to say for yourselves?" he asks them.

They fall down before him. "Nothing, Lord," they cry. "We have sinned."

"I have paid your debt to my father," Emmanuel says, "and I have the power from him to pardon you. And I do pardon you; I pardon you and forgive you completely."

Then he lifts them to their feet, strips them of their mourning clothes, and puts chains of gold about their necks. "And now I have something for you," he says, and he brings forth out of his treasury beautiful robes, glistening white. "These are robes to set you apart," he says, "so that all will know you belong to me. Wear them daily; keep them clean; don't let them drag in the dirt. But if you should sully them, bring them to me quickly so that I may cleanse them again."

Later in the story, those robes did get soiled and did get torn. But they were never *lost,* and in the end, they got patched up and cleaned, so that they could be worn with pride again.

They affected both the standing and the attitude of Mansoul irrevocably. Mansoul could never sin again without pain.

I am affected by attractive clothes. They lift my spirits, buoy me up, and give me a good feeling about myself. If you are this way, too, don't apologize—enjoy them!

Just don't *count* on them, for they could be snatched from you in a flash.

But that robe, glistening white, can never be taken from you. It is your livery, your badge of honor, setting you apart as God's. It will outshine, outlast, and outvalue any other garment, even the most stylish and chic and expensive one you could dream of.

"I will greatly rejoice in the Lord, my soul shall be joyful in my God; for he hath clothed me with the garments of salvation, he hath covered me with the robe of righteousness, as a bridegroom decketh himself with ornaments, and as a bride adorneth herself with her jewels."

Isaiah 61:10

If you're wearing the robe of righteousness, you have a great deal, indeed, to live up to.

9

Prayer Is a Many-Splendored Thing

If an opinion poll could be taken among us Christians regarding prayer, the result would be unanimous.

We're for it.

If a poll could be taken regarding how much time we spend in prayer, most of us would run for cover.

One of the strangest phenomena about prayer is that we spend so much time talking about it and writing about it and reading about it and so little time practicing it.

If anybody could write a book on the pragmatic aspects of prayer, I certainly could, for I have prayed every kind of prayer there is and have made every mistake in the book, a few of which I shall disclose in a moment.

Children who are brought up in an atmosphere of prayer seem to grasp its fundamentals almost from birth. To them, it is a way of life.

Todd (grandson number five) was saying grace along with his schoolmates one day, and after the "amen," his teacher asked him if he knew what *amen* meant. "It means it's time to open my lunch box," he said matter-of-factly, and proceeded to do so. He had asked God's blessing on the food, said, "So be it," left the rest with God in faith, and had gone on with the practical business of living.

Michelle was saying grace one evening at dinner when I was visiting up at the ranch, and among other things, she said, "And thank You, Lord, that Grandmother is here, and—and—just a minute, Lord." She raised her head to me. "Grandmother, are you writing anything now?"

I nodded my head yes.

She went promptly back to business. "Yes, Lord, she is. Please help her with her writing. And don't let her get too tired." And she went on with the rest of it.

After dinner, I went back upstairs, to my work. I had barely settled down when I heard a bloodcurdling scream. It was Michelle. The action from the entire family was immediate. The outside floodlights went on, and every member of the family went bounding out of the house from a different direction. She was hysterical, but we finally got the story out of her. An enormous owl had swooped down from one of the cottonwood trees, grabbed her white kitten in its huge talons, and carried it back up into the tree and out of sight.

The house went on Red Alert; everybody mustered forces and got into action at once. Gary began to bark orders, like a good sergeant should, Mike boosted Sean up the cottonwood tree; Marianne and I stood rooted to the spot. I suddenly thought of my grandmother, who always threw her apron over her head in such moments and

90

waited until the emergency was past. I don't wear aprons, but I must confess I was paralyzed into immobility. (There is one advantage in being a grandmother: You're not expected to shinny up cottonwood trees.) Anyhow, after a few moments of tension, the kitten was dropped into Mike's outstretched hands, and he promptly ran into the house with it. He went to Michelle's room and stopped in the doorway. She was on her knees beside her bed, praying. He tiptoed into the room and stood behind her for a moment, then held the kitten aloft in outstretched arms and dropped it on the bed in front of her. It was unharmed, except for a clump of fur torn out of its back. "You see," he said, "how God has answered your prayers before you even finished praying? 'Before you call, I will answer,' He says."

And they took time out to thank Him; it's their way of life.

Of course children should learn early in life that prayer is not always that simple. It is not some magic formula that grants our every wish and absolves us from all responsibility.

A girl stood up in the college department of Hollywood Presbyterian Church one time and said (without stopping for breath, not even for a comma): "Last week I had a French exam and I was so worried about it and things piled up and I had so many things to do and I asked the Lord to help me and I said 'Lord You've just *got* to help me....'"

Somebody sitting next to me muttered, "Well, I hope you did a little studying, too."

As we grow up, our prayers should get wiser with teaching from the Word of God, and of course, from practice. But often, all too often, they don't.

At least, often *mine* haven't.

Sometimes I have played God in my prayers, when I've had the idea that He might be a little confused and that I had better help Him out.

Once there was someone very close to me, whose ministry was slipping badly, and I was afraid God might not be willing to lift him up, unless I offered Him some sort of bribe. So I instructed Him that I would be willing to have my own ministry slip a notch for every notch He raised this other person up. When neither of these things happened, I seriously questioned whether God was running the universe on schedule.

I did the same thing in praying for my mother. She was facing eye surgery, and the chances were slim that she was going to get through it without going blind. So I bargained with God again. I told Him that I would be willing to lose the sight in one of my eyes, if He would let her keep the sight in one of hers.

I even told Him to hold it off a bit, until I decided which eye I was willing to lose. For weeks I went about the house and drove my car with one eye closed. I practiced in secret, of course. Part of my bargain was that I would never tell a soul how cleverly I had resolved this problem for God. I tried first one eye and then the other, to see which one would afford me the least trouble, and I actually waited expectantly for the light to go out in one eye.

These prayers, masked in the guise of self-sacrifice, just might have been two of the most presumptuous prayers I ever prayed.

Sometimes we pray little, shortsighted prayers, without realizing that they might be a very small part of a "whole other thing."

I did once.

When I first prayed this prayer, naturally I thought I was the center of the universe; the idea that God might have somebody else in mind never occurred to me. What followed was a series of events that looked like *Four Characters in Search of a Plot*, and a long long time elapsed between acts.

The first act began when the children were small. For reasons that are not important enough to go into here, we were forced to live for several months in a very poor section of Philadelphia. It was one of those old, brick, row houses that looked like every other house on the block. It had been cut up into miserably dark apartments, and we were the unhappy occupants of one on the first floor.

The occupants on the floor above us staged an argument every night that turned the air blue with four-letter words, punctuated with crashes of flying crockery and tipped-over furniture. This warfare did not usually start until after the children were asleep. The moment it started, I prayed against their waking up or the plaster ceiling's coming down, whichever was apt to happen first. I prayed every night, far into the night, for God to protect that house for one reason and one reason only—our own safety. I had no vision; indeed, I did not pray beyond my nose. I simply did not want any of us to get hurt. So I covered every crash and every oath—indeed, every *square inch* of that house—with prayer.

This went on for months, until we finally managed to escape and move to a more suitable place.

And so the curtain went down on Act I.

It was many years before the curtain went up on the next act.

Gary and Marianne went to a filmmakers' convention, and it was, of all places, in Philadelphia.

Now Gary has a character trait that must be atavistic; nobody else in the family seems to have it: nostalgia.

I don't think, in all the intervening years, we had ever even mentioned that house.

But once in Philadelphia, he had a sudden yen to go back and see it. So, in a rented car, they drove off to the poor section of Market Street, found the proper block, and by various landmarks remembered from when he was a seven-year-old, he spotted the very house.

He had a sudden yen to go inside and see who was living there. When they got up to the door, the first thing they saw posted over it was a sign: PRAISE THE LORD! There were stickers on the front windows: *Jesus loves you. Have a nice forever.*

The Lord Himself had taken up residence in this very house!

Gary rang the bell with mixed feelings of astonishment and expectancy.

A beautiful black woman opened the door.

"I used to live here, when I was a kid," he said.

"I can't believe it!" she said, staring. Just what she couldn't believe, he was to find out later. She invited him in, and they walked into the very apartment where we had lived!

It turned out that she was an evangelist in a little church around the corner. She had three children in their preteens and early teens—and for months, she'd been fighting a battle to keep their "heads screwed on straight" and their values stable, in this neighborhood where everyone hated authority—and especially hated cops.

She had been praying fervently for God to send her somebody, *from far away and from another culture,* who also loved Jesus, so they could realize they were not fighting the battle alone!

"I'm going to blow your mind," Gary said. "I live about as far away from you as I could and still be in the United States. I'm from California. And I love Jesus.

"And now," he said to the kids, "are you ready for this? I'm a cop."

They were thunderstruck.

The fact that he'd once lived in that very house did not do him any harm; in fact, it paved the way for instant rapport.

The hour that followed was incredible. They made coffee. They sat around and talked—and talked—and talked—and asked questions.

What about authority? the kids wanted to know. Gary

told them it was established by God and showed them Romans thirteen. Could a cop be a Christian? He told them he had managed to be both and hoped to continue to be both, by the grace of God. Being a cop was rough. Being a cop and a Christian was also rough.

Being *anything,* in life, was rough. No matter *what* you were, or *where* you were. But how did he survive and keep his faith, in such an atmosphere?

"Same as you," he said, grinning.

"Through it all," the mother said, "I learned to trust in Jesus. . . ."

And Gary picked it up in song: "Through it all— through it all—I learned to trust in Jesus—I learned to trust in God. . . ." And they all joined in.

In this house!

In this house where I had prayed (with the vision of a goose), not knowing that, thirty-odd years later, a servant of God would be praying for encouragement, for confirmation of her faith, and God would send her a most unlikely man from across the nation— a cop who used to live there!

In all kinds of prayers, there is one common denominator: He delights to surprise us!

But the epitome of prayer is the kind we cannot talk about from personal experience, because it is what it is— secret prayer.

In *Chronicles of Mansoul,* Conscience and Will and Understanding went to the castle in the very heart of Mansoul, to spend some secret time with Prince Emmanuel. He prepared feasts for them—food such as they had never tasted before—imported from his father's country. And he told them marvelous things concerning himself and his father, the great king Shaddai. As they left, he would sometimes put a gift in their hands and whisper, "Tell no one; it is a secret between us."

It was during those secret times that they experienced such love as they had never even dreamed of before. No love had ever been like it, and no other love would be again. To be with him was to satisfy hunger; to be away from him was to be hungry again. . . .

They were transported with joy; they were drowned in wonderment!

Yes, the very highest form of prayer, we cannot talk about from personal experience. If we did, it would be a secret no more.

If you are tempted to "share" your very private prayers in public, beware. You may make yourself look good to your hearers. . . .

But in God's eyes, you've "blown it" (*see* Matthew 6:6).

10

Wanted: Dead or Alive

I had not been at school more than a few weeks, before I realized that I was not cut out to be a nurse. When I phoned my mother and informed her of this fact, she reminded me that, "We always finish what we start, don't we?" So I determined to stick it out for one more week—right up until I passed my state boards, years later.

I was an *A* student, scholastically, but mostly because of a photographic memory. In matters of cause and effect and major premise, minor premise, I was a dunderhead. While the other students were on blood pressures and hypos, I was still trying to find the mercury on the thermometer. When I finally found it, I jumped with astonishment, and the thermometer wound up on the floor, mercury scurrying capriciously in all directions.

With all this in mind, you can imagine my discomfiture (understatement)—terror (fact)—when I was sent up on one of the wards to do what was euphemistically termed "PM care."

"PM care" meant you gave the patient a partial sponge bath, rubbed his back with alcohol, and changed whatever linen was necessary—cheering him the while with bright and comforting chatter and leaving him spruced up, plumped up, propped up, and feeling very good about nurses in general and you in particular.

We were given five patients apiece.

I marched with bravura to my first one. It was a he, and he was behind drawn curtains.

I knew the procedure by heart; I'd been in school a whole month.

I'd practiced on a dummy.

I did not fall into the "And how are we today? Well, now it's time for our PM care" trap. I was far too clever for that.

"Hi," I said instead, and filled his basin and got to work. I had purposed in my heart to be a good nurse and attend to not only my patient's physical needs, but to his emotional needs, as well. So I chattered away happily on the weather and the topics of the day. To all of this, he did not respond. In fact, he did not even look at me—just stared straight ahead.

I was not to be deterred, however. A good and cheerful nurse I was determined to be, at all costs. I mopped him up, rubbed him down, and polished him off with great aplomb.

Through a space in the drawn curtain, I noticed that the man in the next bed was up on one elbow, staring at me quizzically. I gave him a conspiratory look, as if to say,

"Never fear, it takes bit of doing but we can always bring them out of their shells." He responded with what I interpreted as absolute awe at my prowess.

It wasn't until I lifted the basin full of water off my patient's bedside stand that the man on the next bed finally found his voice. "Did you know that man is dead?" he said. "He died ten minutes ago. That's why his curtains are drawn."

I clung to the basin of water as if I expected it to hold me up, but instead it wobbled violently, sending tidal waves splashing over each side alternately, half of it splashing on the floor and the other half of it splashing down the apron of my student uniform. "Oh, yes," I lied brightly, but my smiling muscles were quivering, and so was my voice. "I was just cleaning him up."

I staggered to the utility room and emptied his water, though I'd already emptied half of it on myself. My knees had turned to jelly, my mind was absolutely reeling with shame and horror. Fortunately the man in the next bed had not been assigned to me, so I didn't have to face him again.

I never used this as an illustration from the platform, for it seemed to me so gross and unfeeling that I could see no point in it at all, or how it could ever do anybody any good. For years I did not even think of it; I shoved it down into a morass somewhere in my mind and poked it resolutely under.

It was many years before it surfaced again, and it did so in a most unlikely way. It came to pass, as I waxed older (but not wiser), a woman—with more zeal than good sense—attacked me, right out in plain sight, on the sidewalk, in front of a group of people gathered outside a church. I know now that she was witnessing, but at the time, I thought it was an attack. Anyhow, she grabbed me by the arm and pressed five thin, bony fingers deep into my flesh. And while I was still hurting and unable to escape, she leaned close to me and left a fine spray on my chin as she hissed, "HaveyouacceptedtheLordJesusChristasyourpersonalSaviour?"

"No," I said, nonplussed, "I'm a Republican." Her words were completely foreign to me; I hadn't the faintest idea what she was talking about. I disengaged myself from her grasp and made excuses to get away. *That woman has a very fluid vocabulary*, I thought, as I wiped her spray from my chin and fled.

It wasn't until two years later that I realized what the words had really meant. They were spoken by a substitute minister in the little church I was attending. He had a Scotch brogue so thick I could understand him little better than I had understood that woman. There were two sentences he kept repeating, however, until I began to understand them by virtue of their growing familiarity. "The imporrrrrrtant thing is to be saved," was one. "It's a perrrrrsonal thing," was the other.

Well, that made no sense to me at all, but something was astir within me, and at the end of the service, when the invitation was given, I raised my hand.

I accepted the Lord as my personal Saviour, and I made arrangements to be baptized.

The *personal* business appalled me. It sounded like a valet or something, and very demeaning and too familiar for a God whom I considered very holy and remote and inaccessible—and from whom I intended to keep a respectful distance.

Fortunately for me, a person who knew me as a rascal of the first water dropped in as a self-appointed "elder brother," to poke a few holes in this prodigal.

"You mean to say," she said, patently amused, "that you are going to get dunked in front of all those people and come back up with your hair all wet?" Her voice was derisive now, but something was coming awake in me, so I missed it.

"Oh, no," I said. "As far as I'm concerned, all those people won't even be there. This is a *personal* matter between the Lord and me."

The whole earth seemed to stand still, for it was precisely at that moment that I came alive. I don't know any angel language, but I think a fairly good translation would be that every angel in heaven shouted, *"Gotcha!"*

"I'll make some coffee," I stammered, and I escaped to the kitchen. I put the kettle on and walked over to the venetian blinds that covered the kitchen windows. They were tilted downward against the heat, and I stood there for a moment, my tears going *splat, splat, splat,* running down the slats.

I tilted the blinds open and looked outside.

My God, I thought, *I never knew those pine trees were so beautiful.*

An awareness of God and His love for me came to me with such exquisite clarity, it was like pain. I thought I would die of it.

The teakettle whistled, so I made the coffee and took it back to the living room, but now nothing my "elder brother" could say could puncture me or hurt me. I may have been a brand-new babe, just reborn, but I was all wrapped up in forgiveness, and His banner over me was love.

But another part of my mind was filled with questions: *How had this thing suddenly become real to me? Hadn't I heard all this before? Why had I not been able to understand it?*

It was then that my horrific debacle as a student nurse surfaced again.

That man I had bathed and jabbered at did not respond to me because he could not, and he could not because he was physically dead. I had not been able to respond to the woman who had held me captive and jabbered the most important sentence in life, all in one syllable, because I had been *spiritually* dead.

By what means do we become alive? By being spoken to, or preached at, clearly and effectively—with words pronounced "trippingly on the tongue"?

That can't be it, for Dwight L. Moody could say *Mesopotamia* in one syllable, pronounced *Zacchaeus* "Zachus," and when corrected, cried out, "I don't have *time* to say *Zacchaeus*—there's too much work to be done!"

Yet people were converted by the thousands through his

preaching, and it is said that even people who were walking past the building during his services dropped in their tracks on the sidewalk outside.

Steve Robbins (our pastor at Chapel by the Sea) told once how, right after he "came alive," he was so anxious to witness to people that he rode in a van with some colleagues up and down Sunset Boulevard, buttonholing everybody and anybody they could get to listen. One night he was riding along, reading Scripture to a chap they had invited into the van, and he scarcely knew what he was reading—which was bad enough—but he could read only when they went under a streetlight, which was worse. He, too, said *Mesopotamia* in one syllable, which was worse *yet*.

But when he blurted out, to the chap to whom he'd been reading, "Do you want to accept Jesus as your Saviour?" before he hardly got the words out, the chap shouted "Yes!"

On the other hand, I have been telling a friend about Jesus and quoting Scripture for years now—plainly, explicitly, and prayerfully. She has nodded and agreed with every word I've said, always ending with, "I see what you mean, Ethel. I feel exactly the same way you do. Only you call it God, and I call it luck. So, you see, we are talking about the same thing."

"Let's get one thing straight," I've said. "We are not remotely talking about the same thing. I have a personal relationship. . . ." But I get nowhere.

105

Russell Conwell, who founded the great Baptist Temple and Temple University in Philadelphia, was witnessed to by his aide. He not only did not respond—he scoffed. This was during the Civil War, and it was not until after his aide was killed that Conwell "came alive." He leaned against a tree, looked up into the heavens, and cried out in his soul, "God, I cannot believe in You. My mind won't let me. But I *want* to. If You are *real*—make me aware of You—reveal Yourself to me."

And God did, at that very moment, in a way that Conwell was never able to describe.

He knew he was forgiven.

He knew that he was loved.

And he had never heard about the four spiritual laws. It was not until later that he was able to fill in the gaps.

I was speaking in the Little Church Around the Corner, in New York City, many years ago, at a Jack Wyrtzen rally. At the end of my story, Jack invited those who wanted to give their lives to Christ to come forward. I was supposed to have my head bowed and my eyes closed, but so great was my curiosity that I could not resist leaving one eye open—just a slit.

A sailor, dressed in full uniform, was the first one to come down the aisle, almost on a run.

Now this was many years ago, and I was not used to this invitation business from the platform point of view. So quite naturally I began to swell with pride. I wondered what *I'd* said in *my* message that had made that lad. . . .

"Hold it, Ethel."

It was the Lord's voice, come full-blown into my mind. "Yes, Lord. What is it?"

"That boy's grandmother prayed him into My kingdom before he was even born."

It stopped me in my tracks. My eye snapped shut in a flash, and I never did open it, until after Jack had directed the people into the inquiry room. I never did find out how many people came forward.

Nor have I ever, in any meeting, from that day to this.

As an added precaution, I have never kept track of how many miles I have traveled to speak, or how many times I have spoken. I just don't want to know, for all the glowing statistics and all the "superhype" could be very heady business for me. As I was in school, so I am in life: Academically, I do okay, but in practical Christian living, I'm a dunderhead. If I were to start counting souls and estimating the size of audiences, I could develop the *evangelical-exaggeration syndrome* faster than it would take you to read this.

When it comes to matters of this sort, our specious reasoning knows no limit.

Why, I actually used to think that a standing ovation meant what it *looked* like. Imagine my surprise when I discovered that it takes only one person to start one of those things, compelling everyone in the audience to stagger reluctantly to his feet. Once I thought I had graduated to a spontaneous one, until it dawned on me that at the end of my message, I had raised my arms over my head in praise to God, and my audience, not used to such things, took my gesture as a command to rise. So you can see there is no limit to our foolishness. This heady business is dangerous, because it is so subtle.

You can even make a fool of yourself by veering off in the opposite direction. Many years ago, I was so humble I would not even allow my name to be printed on a program or announced from a platform. Program committees pleaded, reasoned, and cajoled, in vain. "Nay," I demurred sweetly, "to God be the glory. It does not matter who I am. I don't need those ego trips." So, in desperation, someone dubbed me "Story Lady," and I've been stuck with that wretched title ever since. It jolly well serves me right.

I went along on this wise for years, congratulating myself on how spiritual and humble I was, until I remembered something Mark Twain had said: "Don't be so humble; you're not that great."

I didn't need the ego trip? I'd been on an ego trip for years and didn't realize it!

But, proud or humble, the crux is, we carry on our Christian lives and do too much witnessing *on our own strength*. The danger is in becoming discouraged when we are not successful and self-congratulatory when we are.

"Only the Holy Spirit gives eternal life . . ." (John 6:63 LB).

". . . the Spirit alone can give it [the soul] life" (2 Corinthians 3:6 PHILLIPS).

What?

Does this mean we are to leave our witnessing to happenstance? If the Holy Spirit is going to take care of it anyway, why bother?

Well, Jesus Himself cleared that up. "And *you, too,* are witnesses!" He told this to the disciples. And He also meant it for us.

Paul thunders to us down through the ages:

". . . press it home on all occasions, convenient or inconvenient. . . " (2 Timothy 4:2 NEB).

". . . dwelling upon it continually, welcome or unwelcome . . ." (2 Timothy 4:2 KNOX).

I bathed and jabbered at a man, and he did not respond, for he was dead.

A woman witnessed to me, and I did not respond, for I was spiritually dead.

A Scotch minister cried out "It's a perrrrrrrrsonal thing!" and I began to feel the first stirrings of life.

My "elder brother" derided me, and I responded, not to her, but to God.

I realized that salvation was a personal affair between myself and the Lord, and exploded into life.

Then there was Dwight L. Moody. . . .

And my pastor, Steve Robbins. . . .

And Russell Conwell. . . .

And the sailor lad. . . .

No two, the same.

"By My Spirit," saith the Lord.

Remember, the ego trip comes in various and subtle disguises.

11

Childhood Revisited

Revisiting your childhood can be therapeutic, enlightening, shattering, amusing, or life changing, depending on who you are and what part of your childhood you revisit.

A young man told me that he had to go see someone in a hospital once, and he found himself suffused with depression and fear, the moment he walked into the patient's room.

Then he remembered that, as a very small boy, he went to a hospital for a tonsillectomy. A nurse took him and his mother to his room and left them alone for a few minutes. His mother went into the bathroom, and moments later, he heard a strange voice.

"Tommy," the voice said. But there was nobody in the room.

Good grief, it was coming from the wall!

He walked over to the wall and looked up. "Yes, wall," he said, terrified.

"Tommy," the wall said back, "you may get undressed

He spent three days of terror, listening to that spooky wall.

now. And get into bed. I'll be down in a few minutes to take your temperature."

"Okay, wall," he said, and promptly wet his pants.

He didn't tell anyone about his fear, and nobody explained that the voice was coming over an intercom. So he spent three days of terror, listening to that spooky wall, and suffered years of vague dread of hospital rooms.

I know a woman who was pulling out of an emotional breakdown when she went back to her childhood home and discovered that the enormous rooms that had so terrified her, as a child, were little, boxlike rooms you could hardly turn around in.

A man who'd gone back to his childhood haunts discovered that the huge cliff and treacherous rapids he'd been terrified of, as a child, were a little ravine and a creek that was a mere trickle.

But when I went back to visit a part of my childhood, I discovered that the place I was looking for was exactly as I'd remembered it. It wasn't terrifying at all.

I was in a rented car in the city of my childhood, had an afternoon to myself, and decided to snoop into the past. Getting out of the city was a bit of a problem, for there were throughways, now; you didn't just go from the "end of the car line" to a macadam road, as you did back in the days when life was simpler. When I finally got on the right road, though, I knew every bend in it. Even though there were occasional housing tracts and apartment buildings, I could still picture the cornfields and cows and farmhouses that used to be there. When I drew abreast of the spot I

113

was looking for, I pulled off the road and got out of the car, grinning.

There it was, my childhood "castle," set far back from the road, with its own private driveway that went over an arched stone bridge. The once-beautiful landscaping had grown into a jungle of tangled weeds, the giant oaks were choked by ivy that had grown wild, and there was a FOR SALE sign out in front. But everything else was just as I'd remembered it: the great house, with the huge portico on the side; the elaborately carved cornices; the gargoyles projecting from the roof gutters; the many windows; the gazebos; the barns and carriage houses and stables beyond.

Memories came arushing through the filters of my own desires—mostly memories of my mother. I could almost *smell* her standing beside me; not with some exotic scent, for she always smelled just *clean,* like something freshly starched.

I stared at the carriage house, remembering. We had played in it as children, climbing into the ancient (and very valuable) coaches that were stored there. We were allowed to play in them *"Like ladies and gentlemen,* please, and no nonsense." We pretended to be kings and princes and princesses, sitting sedately on the velvet seats, fingering the glass vases that hung on the sides. We sometimes put daisies and buttercups in them. "No water allowed in the vases, please. And no eating inside!" Some of the dramas we played out in those wondrous coaches would strain your imagination. And some of the games we invented in those barns and carriage houses would make your hair stand on end, though I suppose by today's standards, we were surprisingly naive.

It was a long time before I turned to go back to my car. I'd revisited a chunk of my childhood, and it was exactly as I remembered it, except for one thing.

It wasn't my house.

I'd been allowed there only to play with the two children who lived there and with whom I went to school.

I got back in the car and turned to look again. The windows of the great house stared back at me vacantly, without welcome, like faceless, voiceless ghosts. I suddenly realized as an adult what I had never noticed as a child.

I had never—not once—been invited inside.

"Why didn't you tell me?" I said aloud, to my long-dead mother. "Why didn't you tell me that, compared to those people, we lived on the wrong side of the tracks? Our houses were always scrubbed and freshly painted, we always had a lovely little garden, we had enough to eat. Why didn't you tell me that you were struggling alone to bring us up? Why did you tell us we were all *happy* and *advantaged*?"

"I didn't say *happy* or *advantaged*, Ethel. I said *blest*."

"It's the same thing."

"It is not the same thing, Ethel, and you know it. For that matter, why didn't you tell your sons that you were struggling to bring *them* up alone, or that, compared to some people, *they* lived on the wrong side of the tracks? Why did you tell them they were advantaged—eh, blest?"

I couldn't think of an answer, so I got in the car and drove on.

About a half mile down the road, this came full-blown into my mind: "Seest thou a man diligent in his business? he shall stand before kings . . ." (Proverbs 22:29).

The sense of the presence of my mother was gone. All that was left was a clean odor in the car, like something freshly starched.

She always did have the last word.

12

Sometimes Animals Behave Like People

I'm not trying to be facetious, but from my long years of observation, it seems to me that animals behave a lot like people. Of course, we have been compared with sheep in the Bible, and sheep are just about the dumbest animals God ever created—except turkeys, and they're birds.

At the risk of being cloyingly sentimental, I'll come right out and say that I am an animal lover. I don't mean that I talk baby talk to them, or sit them up in my best overstuffed chair and feed them dainty morsels of meat by hand, or buy them rhinestone collars, or rush them to the vet every time they sneeze. I just find them heartwarming and companionable and amusing—more amusing than many people I have met. When my children were growing up, we always had pets, for I had read somewhere that one should not bring up children without animals; it's bad for their psyches.

After the children left, I lived for years in apartments and traveled a great deal, so the idea of pets never occurred to me. But when I bought a house, I decided to have them again. It would be good for when the grandchildren came around, I told myself. I didn't want to come right out and say pets might be good for *my* psyche.

In any case, I began to observe animals again, and I discovered something very interesting, which I shall tell you about later.

I could fill a book with the animals I've known, but for now I shall mention only three.

First there was Mr. Cat.

My first conversation with Mr. Cat was planned to establish our relationship (me boss-him slave), and would, of course, be rigged in my favor.

"Cat," I said, for I had not yet named him, "I have just been reading an article in *Lois* magazine about a cat named Fenica, who belongs to Rexella Van Impe and travels all over the country with her." Cat looked the other way. "She *travels*," I repeated, "on airplanes and stays in hotels. And she accepts a *leash*, just like a dog."

Cat dug at his hide for a moment, then walked out of the room.

"I hate to fracture your future," I said, following him, "but compared with Fenica, you are a total failure, and I expect you to shape up."

He gave me a gelid stare.

The first time I saw that stare was the day I brought him home from Gary's ranch. I didn't really want a cat, but I'd been finding mysterious toast crumbs in my kitchen cupboards and drawers. As I never made toast in those places,

I thought this was strange—until Gary dropped by one day and fished in my silverware drawer for a spoon. He informed me that those were not toast crumbs.

Some mice had moved in to share my home.

Cat spent his first day with me sitting on the hood of my car, staring at me with huge, yellow eyes. He was white with black marks on his back that reminded me of huge inkblots, so I finally stopped calling him Cat and named him Rorshach.

We weren't too far into our orientation period when I realized that it was going to be more difficult than I'd thought. When I called him, he ignored me, unless it involved food. When I scolded him or whacked him for a misdemeanor, he spent the rest of the day on a neighbor's roof, glaring at me when I went out to my upstairs deck.

Things took a turn for the better after the mice moved out. The pickings were slim, and Rorshach began to realize that I was buying the food. After all, money does talk. He would lie in wait for me when I came downstairs and leap at me playfully. He would climb up the open stairway to the balcony on the *underside* of the carpeted steps, to get my attention. I began to invent different names for him. I called him Mr. Cat when I was being stern, Pretty Kitty when I felt affectionate. And he was Flasher when he leaped from the balcony down into the living room, onto my head, to the top of a love seat, to the fireplace mantle, just like a stone being scaled across a pond. I began to wonder who was "shaping up" whom.

Then one night I was lying down in the den, reading,

and he climbed up on my chest and began to slap at the pages. It got increasingly difficult to read, so I decided to divert him with a snack. As he followed me, purring, out to the kitchen, I thought I heard him chuckle.

And then I knew.

The "shaper" was Rorshach; the "shapee" was Ethel.

Then there was Heidi. Heidi was a ginger Doberman. I got her when she was a pup. She was beautiful; her coat was like brown satin, and she moved with the grace of a ballerina.

I've known some hyperactive children, but I never heard of a hyperactive dog, until I met Heidi. She could do just about anything you'd expect an intelligent pup to do, except buckle under to authority. She came from a royal family, and apparently she knew it. Her grandfather was Dictator Von Glenhugel, who was in *Who's Who of Doggery,* and the mere mention of his name made all the Dobermans in the world pause for a moment of silence. Somehow I think Heidi found this out. I think she must have read her papers over my shoulder, for she could cuddle, she could love, she could be amusing, she could, in fact, do everything but go along with the nonsense rules that were made for the *hoi polloi* of dogdom.

I had her ears cropped, so they would stand straight and tall and majestic. After all, nobody wants a Doberman whose ears look like the ears of a beagle. If you're going to have a Doberman, do it right. While her ears were still bandaged, I told her explicitly to leave them alone. I told her this each time I tucked her in the garage for the night.

But in the dead of night, she would wake up and hurl herself against the kitchen door. For some reason, she always led with her left ear. That ear was rebandaged by the vet more times than I care to admit. But when the whole, horrible ordeal was over, it still did not stand up straight. The only way I could get it to do so was to run her *north* on the beach, so the west wind would blow it up. But when I turned around and we ran south again, down it would go.

The ear cropping was a dismal failure. I had a Doberman of noble lineage who looked like any common dog of the *hoi polloi!*

I didn't mind that so much. What I minded was that she would not subject herself to training. I'd been trying to train her from babyhood, but toilet training was just about all she would subject herself to.

So I called upon Gary to come down and straighten her out. He put her through a training program that was so rigorous, I turned my head in horror and seriously considered reporting him to the SPCA. But when he was finished, she was obedient to his every command. The most surprising thing was that she still *liked* him.

Then he put us through our paces together. I took the choke chain. "Heidi, stay," I practiced, and "Heidi, heel."

Every order I gave her (under Gary's supervision) she obeyed.

Right up until he left the premises.

"Heidi, heel!" I said sternly, as I started for the beach, hand firmly gripping her leash, which was attached to her choke chain. She leaped joyfully forward with such speed

121

I was not her master, and she knew it.

that I imagined a jet stream must be pouring out behind us. "Heel!" I cried, jerking on her choke chain. "Heel!" But she kept going with such strength that I dug my heels into the ground and plowed furrows all the way to the beach. I did not look like a woman walking a dog; I looked like a woman trying to water-ski on land. Once at the beach, she would race toward unsuspecting people in the distance, dragging me behind her, crying, "Heidi, STAAAAY!" Strong men would blanch, sink in their tracks, and say their last-minute prayers. I tried to explain that she was not attacking, she was just playful. Well, now, it's very difficult to explain to people half-dead with fright that the huge Doberman rushing toward them is merely playful. So I became very unpopular on the beach. Fortunately that section of the beach was semiprivate, so I could choose times when it was practically deserted to run her.

Meanwhile, I got son Gary back again, to substantiate the training he'd given her—sort of like a booster shot. She was splendid all the time he was there. But after he left, even though I did (or thought I did) everything that he had done, she went on with her exuberant ways, scaring everybody half to death.

No matter how hard I tried, I was not her master, and she knew it. She would love me, she would amuse me, she would give me lip service (if dogs could talk), but she would not obey me. My commands fell on deaf ears.

So—after much dallying and postponing—I made the decision! Heidi had to go.

Both of my sons were already overcrowded with Dobermans and Great Danes; she would have to go elsewhere. *But to just the right home,* I thought, *where she could have a safe place to run off some of that excess energy.*

The right offer finally came from a psychiatrist who lived in a beautiful home on the Pacific Palisades. His house was surrounded by an enclosed acre of ground, and I could not turn his offer down.

The day he called for her, I said good-bye, and as she went out the front door, I went out the back, to the garage; I did not want to see her actually leave and get into his car. I drove off in the opposite direction, to the post office. "A psychiatrist and a looney dog," I muttered. "They deserve each other." But it did not help. I swallowed big lumps of grief all the way.

I have been guilt ridden about that dog ever since.

Then there is Pokey. Pokey is pure *hoi polloi.* She is the daughter of a pedigreed collie and a pedigreed boxer. Her prestigious parents had somehow flown their coops one night and got together. Pokey was the product of this clandestine tryst.

There is no way to describe Pokey. She is just a nothing dog. Her legs are too short, and her collie nose is somewhat snubbed by her boxer heritage. But she has the eyes of a fawn, ringed with dark hairs that have made me accuse her more than once of having gotten into some eyeliner. That face encompasses all the love of dogdom.

She is a moody dog. Periodically she puts herself on a fast and just hangs around the house and mopes, or if I try to run her on the beach, she drags her feet, walking behind me like a reluctant child being taken to the dentist. I understand her bad days; she understands mine. But most important, I think, is the fact that she obeys.

"Pokey, I can't take you with me this time, so stay," I say as I back out of my garage and press the remote control to close the door. My last sight of her is of a desolate dog, her tail between her legs, her nose pressed against the washer-dryer. She ignores the bone I've left her. She is not interested in eating; she is interested only in being with me. I know that when I get back, she will come to meet me, bent double into a horseshoe, her tail wagging against her nose. Then she will leap upon her bone, and from there to her water, and from there to her food. She is willing to get on with life, now that I am back.

Actually, Pokey has been with me through both Heidi and Mr. Cat. She has tolerated them and watched them with resignation, as they took over my life. But they have come and gone—and Pokey stays on.

She is not beautiful, and she has no pedigree, but she has the one ingredient in her personality that surpasses these attributes: She is obedient to my commands.

"But animals?" you cry. "You're comparing us with *animals?* Why, you can't even compare us with other ordinary *people?* We're born-again Christians!"

Yes.

So am I.

So was Mansoul. In *Chronicles of Mansoul,* after Mansoul invited Prince Emmanuel into the city, the chief officers—Conscience and Will and Understanding—began to take him for granted.

Not all at once.

It was slow.

It was subtle.

Satan is crafty.

They became enamored of Mr. Carnal-Security (confidence in the flesh), and they began to fall prey to all the little sins, the "acceptable" sins Christians allow themselves. They masked their shortcomings with great spirituality and words of great pith and moment. They became manipulative, they became headstrong—and they became sulky. It was a long time before they became aware that the sense of presence of their prince was no longer with them. It was a rude awakening, and it was a long, weary way back to him.

When I say that some animals behave like people, I am saying that I am a combination of the three animals I've just told you about. Sometimes I'm like Mr. Cat, manipulating God, hoping that I'll bring Him around to my way of thinking. Sometimes I'm like Heidi, going joyously on ahead of Him, working for Him, paying Him lip service—doing everything but *obeying* Him. And sometimes I'm like Pokey, loving *and obeying* but sometimes—no, often—sulking. I guess, of these three pets, Pokey comes closest to the real love relationship between slave and master. She would rather be with me than eat. She would rather be with me than do anything else that might tempt her away.

But she sulks.

I have said many things to Christ in my prayers, and He

has given me many different answers, but whenever I cry out to Him, "I love You," the answer always comes back, before I hardly get the words out: "If ye love me, keep my commandments" (John 14:15).

I know what He means; how well I know what He means.

Remember the sheep. A sheep can stray from its master and *eat* its way to the edge of a cliff and topple over. And although the turkey isn't scriptural, I cannot leave him out, for he can raise his beak to the sky in a hard rain and *drown*—within a few feet of shelter!

Now that I've written myself into a corner, I'll have to come right out and admit I was wrong. Animals don't behave like people.

It's the other way around.

People sometimes behave like animals.

13

Don't Dent My Bubble

I was surprised when I found out I was walking around in a bubble.

We'd always been taught that each of us needed a certain amount of *space* around us, and that when other people invaded our space, we became quite defensive. It's the psychological aspect of the old "territorial imperative" business. It's very strong in animals, and they are quick to let any invader know that he is trespassing and that he's about to get hurt, if he doesn't move on.

The three-spined sticklebacks handle the matter in a most sensible way. These pugnacious little fish live in our northern sea inlets, and to my knowledge, have never had a real knock-down-drag-'em-out fight. If they meet at the invisible border of their spaces, they swim toward each other, then stop, glaring at each other furiously, eyeball-to-eyeball, a quarter of an inch apart. There they stay for a moment, quivering from stem to stern with rage, and then vent their spleen by diving to the bottom and digging holes in the sand with their noses.

Then, all their anger spent, each one swims calmly back into his own space.

We are forced to be more subtle. We have to learn to keep other people out of our "spaces" by our wits.

Only now, the spaces are called *bubbles*.

I rather fancy the idea of bubbles, myself; they sound secure and protective. I'll say right off that I don't want anyone getting inside my bubble, unless it is in the specific will of God. If it is not, I don't want anybody to even *dent* it.

In connection with this, I have a hard time with those Sunday-morning services when, during prayer time, we are asked to go to one other person and confess our problems, faults, and/or sins to him, and in return listen to his. I'm not the least bit *critical* about this; actually *scared stiff*, is what I am. I can barely manage to say grace without weeping. I think in an evening service, I might be able to handle it, but I have been in the very-structured morning services of the Presbyterian Church for too much of my life, to handle such intimacy in broad daylight. I don't relish the idea of going up to a stranger, or even a friend, and confessing my sins. I have a difficult enough time admitting them to God. And although I might have a compassionate interest in someone else's problems, I haven't the faintest curiosity about his *sins*.

Therefore, I usually sit, my head bowed, the sweat dripping off my nose, hoping that nobody will come at me with the intent that we will swap our deepest and most private affairs and secrets.

It may seem like a paradox that I can talk to ten thousand people without a quiver, but I can't talk to one person about private matters without being terrified, or without the desire to cry. My nose begins to twitch, my jaw begins to wobble, and my face gets all out of shape.

I did give it a try once, in a morning service. I walked over to a woman who had raised her hand earlier in the service, indicating she was a visitor. I put my hand on her shoulder and prayed fervently for her, my voice hitting three notes on every syllable. Afterward she said stiffly, "Thank you for your nice little prayer," turned on her heel, and walked out. I realized that what I had lacked in discernment I had more than made up for in crass effrontery. I had, uninvited, dented her bubble, when I hadn't a clue to what was going on in her heart.

It reminded me of a time some years back, when I had been sitting in the front row of the morning service of Hollywood Presbyterian Church. A few feet away from me was a huge bowl of the most enormous yellow chrysanthemums I had ever seen in my life.

As we said the Apostles' Creed, I found myself staring into one of them.

"I believe in God the Father. . ." we began.

And my mind stopped right there.

The unfathomable mystery of that *one flower*—and He created the *universe!*

I was so filled with wonder that I thought my very heart was going to burst.

"And in Jesus Christ, His only Son. . . ."

Oh, good grief, I was going to cry. I felt it welling up in me. I was not going to cry dainty tears, either. I was going to cry in big, gulping sobs that I would not be able to control.

I fled from the sanctuary, hoping I could hold back until I could escape, and cursing myself for having sat in the front seat in the first place.

I barely got out the door when a woman caught up with me and stopped me in the corridor and began to commiserate with me about my deep and terrible sin. It only made me cry harder.

I finally disentangled myself, thanked her, and went back out to my car. I didn't have the heart to tell her that not only did I not have a problem, but I was so filled with joy I could have floated all the way home.

It made me think of the time my aunt Ethel (they differentiated between us by calling her "big Ethel" and me "little Ethel," which confused us all, after I got to be bigger than she was) went to a funeral. The women rode in the carriages while the men walked solemnly alongside, which was the custom in those days. Only it didn't make any sense to her, because it was raining hard outside—it was a regular deluge. But the men were trudging along outside, the rain dripping off their hats, and the women were inside the carriages—with their *umbrellas*. This was so patently ridiculous that she began to laugh to herself about it. She tried to hide her merriment behind a handkerchief, and everyone thought she was crying. But the more they comforted her, the harder she "cried." For years afterward, no one could understand her uncontrollable grief over the loss of someone she barely knew.

We seldom know what is really on another person's heart.

"But Matthew 18:19," we cry. "What about that?"

Yes, what about that? "Again I say unto you, That if two of you shall agree on earth as touching any thing that they shall ask, it shall be done for them of my Father which is in heaven."

If I remember my teaching correctly, the crux of this verse is in the word *agree*. And *agree*, in this case, means "in harmony with": two people in harmony with each other, both understanding exactly what they are asking and why. It also means two people in harmony with God—both understanding that they are asking something in His will and through the Holy Spirit.

An orchestra plays, or should play, in harmony. The instruments are different, and they are playing different notes, but somehow it all goes together. They *agree*. And they know all the facts.

On the other hand, our specious reasoning knows no limits, when it comes to leaving pertinent facts out of our prayer requests.

One time, a woman asked me to pray with her about a husband.

She wanted one: a particular one.

It seemed reasonable enough, except for one little problem. She had not considered a vital fact. The husband she wanted was separated from, but still very much married to, his present wife. If I had agreed to pray with her about this matter, she would have been playing the violins in the wrong key, and I would have been playing the kettledrum.

All of this is not to say that we are not to pray together. But there is a difference between indiscriminately walking up to another person to confess or to pray and feeling a strong compulsion to do so. When it is done by the Spirit of God's leading, it is glorious.

Twice, this has happened to me during a morning service. Once, a strange woman came to tell me not to be discouraged, that God had not forgotten me, that He had forgiven me, that He would see me through this crisis. "I *never* do this sort of thing," she said, her voice shaking, "but the Lord wouldn't let me stay in my seat. And when somebody as timid as I am comes clear across the church to speak to you, it *must* be of the Lord."

She had been definitely led by the Spirit of God, for I had needed that encouragement that day, that hour, that very moment.

Another time, a woman came to me just to tell me she loved me!

She made my day! Ah, love—pure, unadulterated, *agape* love. This is one area in which you *can't* make a mistake.

But, do you know, I can't even seem to do *this* properly. The more sincere I am about it, the more difficult it is, and the more weepy I feel. On my way to deliver some tapes of a manuscript to the lovely gal who was transcribing them for me, I got thinking about her and her terrific husband.

They had been a couple of happy beach kids, without goal or purpose, until one day they read *The Seven Levels of Heaven*. Being both intelligent and curious, they went to the library and checked out a Bible—not as the Word of God, but as just another book, to compare with what *The Seven Levels of Heaven* had to say.

So now they had the Word of God in their home.

When it came time to return the Bible, they renewed it, instead, then finally bought one of their own. They read it avidly, first as a book, to satisfy their intellectual curiosity, then as something else, which stirred strange longings in their hearts.

They decided it would do no harm to say grace at the table. Then they decided it might be a good thing to try going to church.

And *then*, one of the chapel pastors ran into them on the beach and witnessed to them. It was done not only with expertise, but with discernment and the power of God. It wasn't long afterward that they opened the door Christ had been knocking on and let Him in.

Now they had not just the Word of God in their home, but God Himself in their hearts, in the person of Jesus Christ.

In the next few years, though their problems and troubles abounded, the grace of God did much more abound, and spiritually they got richer and richer.

I was thinking about them both, as I drove along, and I began to talk aloud to them. "Leah," I said, "I have watched you and Bill from the first Sunday you ever walked into the chapel, and I have never told you how much your lives have meant to me. You have grown from spiritual babes to spiritual giants. Look at you! You the church secretary, Bill an elder. Everything about you both is radiant. You light up my life! There are no words to tell you what a blessing you've been to me."

Which words turned out to be prophetic, for when I got there to deliver the tapes, there *were* no words.

I was tongue-tied.

I gave her the tapes, asked how she was coming with the typing, told her to phone me from home if she had any questions, and even threw in a "Have a nice day" before I escaped to my car and headed for home.

"Why didn't you tell her?" God asked.

"I meant to, Lord. You know I meant to."

"Then why didn't you do it? Why did you withhold that little cup of cold water from her?"

"Because when I was thinking about her and Bill on the way down, I got so choked up with love. You know what would have happened: My nose would've begun to twitch, my jaws would've wobbled, and my face would've gotten all out of shape."

"You are a devout coward."

"I promise, Lord. The very next tape I take to her, I'll tell her."

I did. And my nose twitched and my jaws wobbled and my face got all out of shape. But I sang all the way back home.

I got my bubble dented.

Maybe those who get their bubbles dented the most live the best.

I'm working on it.

14

Peace and Quiet and Other Hazards

Next to diets, articles about how to find peace and quiet, or how to get out of a rut, probably sell more magazines than a condensed story by Barbara Cartland. If you don't believe this, ask any young mother at the end of a hard day. I am not a young mother, but I do belong to a species that has peace and quiet high on the wish list. I am a writer, or thought I was, until I heard someone say, "Anyone who has half a mind to write a book, writes a book." So now I'm not so sure.

Anyhow, a while back I was enjoying a writing block when Gary and Marianne told me the way to both get out of my rut and get some peace and quiet was to come up to their small ranch in the mountains. They had an apartment upstairs with a fireplace and an outside entrance. They had promised me that for as long as I could get up the stairs, I could have it to myself. It was a standing invitation. So I packed my car with my typewriter and tape recorder and my dog Pokey and Mr. Cat, and headed for the ranch.

I had never met the geese before.

This is a jolly idea, I thought, as I drove up there. *Peace and quiet. No telephone calls. No one tempting me out for lunch or dinner. No drop-in visitors.*

This is a jolly idea indeed, I thought two hours later, as I turned into the lane that led to the house. The house was huge and rambling, shaded by giant, ancient cottonwood trees. Here I would be safe and snug, cooled by the breezes if the weather was warm, warmed by wood fires if the weather got chilly. But more important than either of these, I would have peace and quiet. I stopped the car gratefully and opened the door.

Marianne wasn't about, at the moment.

But the geese were.

I had known about the ducks, but I had never met the geese before. They came at me, hissing and squawking, their heads lowered, their necks wagging slowly from side to side. By the time I realized that it was not a welcome but an attack, I barely had time to get back in the car. A few minutes later, it was apparent that they had no intentions of letting me out of it.

But I had no intention of sitting there and waiting for rescue, thwarted by *geese.* I fished a record album out from the backseat to use as a shield, and headed for the house.

That was when the dogs came.

They were enormous ginger Dobermans. They came at me, not to attack, but to welcome me. I'd known them since they were born. A couple of years before, Gary and his family had asked me to care for their very pregnant

141

Dobe while they went on vacation. I had agreed; I knew the dog; she was no problem.

She was no problem, but she was off schedule. She decided to deliver two weeks early, under a neighbor's beach house.

Under it.

Whereupon Sean and I had gone down there, armed with a pound of hamburger and a pair of oven mitts, and dug them all out—eleven of them.

These two Dobes had called me Mother ever since. They welcomed me with leaps of joy, and getting to the house was a battle to keep my footing. Marianne showed up eventually, and I unpacked my car and went joyfully upstairs.

The next morning the folks were gone, and I settled down to work.

That was when one of the pigs got out.

Now, I have never been on speaking terms with a pig, or even had a nodding acquaintance. I went downstairs and, arms flapping, tried to shoo him back into the pen, but he quickly got out of my range. I chased him around the yard a bit, then remembered that pigs sometimes get heart attacks when they are frightened or run too fast, so I gave up and let him alone. I reasoned that he was so fat he wouldn't get very far.

Once upstairs, I stood gazing out of the window, and witnessed a little drama which I know you will not believe, for I did not believe it, either.

A hen came bounding out of some tall ivy, her feathers

ruffled, and galloped—*galloped*—toward a rooster who happened to be passing by.

"Pauuuuuk!" she squawked in his ear.

"Paauk?" he said, horrified.

She let loose with "paauks" and "puks" through which, although I did not understand them, I perceived that some sort of hanky-panky had gone on in that tall ivy.

"Paughgggr," he growled, and bounded into the ivy. There ensued a battle which, though I did not see it, I concluded that it was so, for the ivy flew and the feathers flew and the squawks were horrible to hear. The rooster came out, triumphant, and went back to the hen, whispering "paauks" of comfort into her ear.

Then *another* rooster emerged, tail drooping, and ran for cover. (I learned later that this particular hen belonged to this particular rooster who had been passing by, and he was not about to let another rooster invade his territory.)

I stood there a moment, marveling at the ways of animals and birds and thinking vaguely about the territorial imperative, and finally went happily back to work, in peace and quiet.

That was when the bull got out.

He won't be any trouble, I thought, as I hurried downstairs. *He's only two weeks old—a mere bottle-fed babe.* And he had a short length of rope around his neck; it would be easy. I knew the psychology of leading animals like that, anyhow. I'd heard about the little milkmaid who, when three strong men had been unable to budge a cow, had put her fingers in the cow's mouth and led her back into her stall. I would do the same.

"Come on, baby," I crooned softly, as I took hold of the rope and started to stick my finger in his mouth. But he took my whole hand and began to suck on it with force that threatened to get not only my hand, but my arm, up to the elbow. "Come on, baby," I kept crooning, "Come on, baby," pulling on the rope and gently tugging him back toward his stall. But it soon became apparent that he was no cow and I was no little milkmaid. He was as big as a small horse and twice as frisky. He veered. He zigged. He zagged. He leaped into the air, me flying after him like the tail on a kite. Fifteen minutes later, sweating and panting, I managed to get him back in his pen. It was then I remembered that the milkmaid had dipped her fingers into her pail of milk before she had put them into the cow's mouth.

It took a shower and a cup of tea to get me back to work. And it took awhile to get back in the mood, but with a great effort, I finally did.

That was when the goat got out.

This goat was not a family goat. I'd never seen him before. He was a neighbor's billy, who had been invited over to stay awhile and perchance to mate with one of the ranch nannies. But, as it turned out, he had been interested in everything but mating. I did not know this at the time. I just thought he was one of the family. So I dropped my work and went down the stairs.

The little milkmaid story had taught me nothing about goats, so I certainly did not intend to put my finger in his mouth and croon, "Come on, baby." I intended to grab him by one horn and march him back in the pen, and no nonsense. But as I walked toward him and he dug his front feet into the ground and lowered his head, I decided promptly that discretion was the greater part of valor, and turned and bolted back up the stairs, him after me. It turned out—happily—that though he was a formidable foe on level ground, he was not so great on stairs. I made it well ahead of him and got back into my quarters.

I must confess I was not feeling altruistic at this point. I just left him alone. I didn't care if he tore up the place or ran away and never came back.

When the family returned, Gary put him back and inspected the gate. There was no way he could have gotten out; he must have jumped the fence. It seemed that he had figured out how to do everything but mate.

I spent the evening with the family, downstairs. "And how did your writing go today, Grandmother?" they asked me.

So I told them.

"Oh, well," Marianne said, "an empty stable is always clean."

I looked at her in silence, trying to comprehend.

"When there are no oxen in it," she explained matter-of-factly. "I found that in Proverbs."

Then the children entertained us with skits.

Michelle climbed up on a tall, antique file cabinet and stood there giggling, a sheet wrapped around her head. Then Sean came into the room and knelt before her and cried, "Rapunzel, Rapunzel, let down your hair!" Where-

upon she let go of an end of the sheet and let it drop, and
came tumbling down with it.

I can't remember what the other skits were. I only know
they got crazier.

But their prayers, afterward, were earnest and filled
with thanks, mostly for belonging to that family!

"Thanks for everything," I said as I left. "And good
night, oxen."

Once upstairs in my inner sanctum, I looked up *oxen*. It
was in Proverbs 14:4: "Where no oxen are, the crib is
clean: but much increase is by the strength of the ox."

"Close enough," I muttered.

The next day was Saturday. There was to be a parade in
the local village. Would I go? Well, the Barretts were in it,
riding their prize horses. Sean was driving an antique
wagon that he had been lovingly restoring for months. In
the back of the wagon, Gary was to sit on a stool and milk
one of the nannies. How could I possibly *not* go?

I drove over to the village, well ahead of parade time
and parked my car in a strategic place, to watch. When I
saw them coming, I sprang out of my car and joined the
crowd at the edge of the road. As they came near us, I exclaimed, "These are my children and grandchildren!
When they get here, be sure to cheer and clap!" Everyone
exclaimed what a clever family arrangement that was—
especially the chap sitting on the stool in the back of the
wagon, milking the goat. But as they got abreast of us,
Gary aimed one teat at us and squeezed. With unerring ac-
curacy, the stream of milk shot out and got me in the eye,

and what was left over splattered on the chap standing next to me.

"That guy's your son?" he asked, mopping his face.

"Yes," I said grimly, "and he's not getting anything for Christmas."

The following week, there was a teachers' convention, which was a delight to the grandchildren, as they were home from school. Its advantages to me were questionable, however. They'd been told not to interrupt me, so they did not come upstairs. But they did not need to; their voices carried over hill and dale; the ranch was surrounded by mountains, and the acoustics were fantastic. Their ordinary conversation sounded like the mating call of a lawn mower. Their wit was astonishing. Their energy knew no bounds.

Personally, I think it is Marianne's fault. She comes from a family that has produced nothing but pastors and doctors and musicians. They have been known for generations for their scholarship and their wit and their talent, but they have never been known for being quiet. Spending a holiday weekend with them necessitates at least a week of rest, before and after.

Inasmuch as I am known for my gentle ways, soft, rippling laughter, and long silences, I can only conclude that those lively genes in the McBain family have gravitated down through her and thence to my grandchildren. Much of their behavior was undoubtedly atavistic, from the McBain side; they never got it from me.

Actually, I enjoyed all this, but I wasn't getting much

work done. This homestead was one of pure, unadulterated chaos. It was noisy. It was incredibly cluttered, with canvases and paints, unfinished games of chess, books opened at strategic places, hooked rugs in the making, charcoal sketches on easels—and everything with a sign on it: Do Not Disturb.

I could hardly wait for the day, a few days hence, when I had a speaking date and could escape. When the day came, I left Pokey and Mr. Cat behind and headed for home, to pick up my mail and change before going on. During the drive, I thought of how good it would be to get home. I thought so right up until I drove into my garage.

There was no Pokey to greet me, bent double like a horseshoe, her tail wagging frantically against her nose. There was no Mr. Cat to jump down from a shelf and come running. I went into the house—and stopped.

As I am the sort of a bore who keeps even my spices in alphabetical order, everything was in its place. My cleaners had been there, so everything was also spotless. It was so clean it squeaked.

But it was empty.

There had been no question about who was to clean the fireplaces, feed the animals, bring in the wood, clean the bathrooms, load the dishwasher, or gather the eggs. There were no animals, and my cleaners had taken care of the rest.

I opened all the shutters, to let the light in. I let the physical light in, but I could not let something else in. Something was missing.

The oxen.

After two silent and sterile days, I drove back to the ranch, to continue my writing. Each time I opened my upstairs door for any reason, I was greeted by the two enormous Dobermans, an assortment of very aggressive cats, and a goat named Mushroom. The mean billy had been returned to the neighbor from whence he came, but not before he had taught Mushroom to jump the fence. They were all exceedingly sociable and uninhibited, and barged into the living room before I could blink, until I learned to open the door with extreme caution. As I was shooing them out for the third time, I took a moment to look down at the stables. The children were saddling their horses. "Daisy's about to foal. Maybe tonight," Sean called up.

"Be sure the baby presents its front feet first and its head down," I called back. "If it doesn't, Daisy's in trouble." He looked up at me admiringly. Actually I'd gotten my veterinarian's expertise from reading James Herriot's *All Things Wise and Wonderful.*

A few days later, it looked as if the end of my book was in sight. But I decided to stay over a few more days, to relax in this wildly beautiful place. I brewed myself some coffee and started down the stairs with a cup, to give Marianne the good news. (I have a blind spot when it comes to my daughters-in-law; I like them.)

We met each other halfway. "I was just coming up to have my coffee with *you,*" she said.

I opened my mouth to say, "I've decided to stay," when I looked past her, toward my car. One of the goats had decided to sleep in late. On my car—*on* it.

He was curled up on the hood, snoring happily, with no idea of the trouble he was about to get into.

"I've decided to go home," I said. "I'm nearly finished." Which I was.

The goat took off, with my assistance, and I took off for home, to recover from my attack of peace and quiet.

That night I got a call from Sean. "Daisy foaled, Grandmother," he said. "And I watched her closely. The filly presented her feet first with her head down. Yup—she's a filly, and she's beautiful, with a white star on her forehead. I named her Far-out."

"Oh," I said from my clean stall, "that's wonderful!" I went back to my peace and quiet.

I had barely healed when Steve phoned from Texas. "Mother," he said, "we have an idea. Why don't you come down here for some peace and quiet? You could stay over for Thanksgiving."

The wheels in my head began to go around. I remembered a visit there last summer. I was to go down there and do some writing in peace and quiet. My study would be their huge and lovely backyard. My roof would be the spreading canopy of ancient pecan and apricot trees. The lawn furniture was the best, and very comfortable.

But they had a couple of turkeys, a tom and a hen. And Tom was about the meanest turkey I have ever met. He was meaner than the neighbor's billy goat and all the mean geese put together. He hated me on sight. I was not about to walk in his yard and sit on his lawn furniture, if he could help it; he would not let me off the back porch.

But I had a weapon: a commodious purse—one of those "organized" purses that women carry when they travel. I never went off the porch without it. I would hold it against my thighs, and when he came rushing forward to attack me, I batted him in the beak with it. We never did make friends.

I thought of the oxen down there in Steve's homestead. It would be really nice to see my grandchildren—but Tom?

A very unworthy thought came to my mind. A mischievous gleam came into my eye. "I'll come down," I said to my son, "when you send me a picture of Tom, legs *up*, ready for the oven."

It turned out that I could not go down, but I've been assured that it was just as well; Tom was as tough in death as he'd been in life.

Last weekend the clan from the ranch presented themselves at my front door. They were down to the beach for surfing.

"Hi, Grandmother," they all said in a chorus. "Your oxen are here!" Somehow their voices did not sound as loud: must be the terrific acoustics up there in those mountains.

We had a great weekend together, and as they left, they called out, "Come up soon as you can, for some peace and quiet!"

"I sure will!" I called back.

And I meant it.

After all, there were five horses that had not jumped the

fence. And a dozen ducks that had swum placidly on the pond, minding their business. And one bull that hadn't got out. And two prize 4-H sheep. And three nannies. And three pigs.

And I'd been up there some weeks when *nobody* kicked over the traces.

Maybe it was just a freak week.

"I sure will!" I called again, as they drove away. "Good-bye, oxen!"

Are you yearning for peace and quiet? Hang in there, young mothers. Some day, God willing, you will have a choice. Peace and quiet, or a stall full of oxen, whichever you desire, and at times of your own choosing.

It's the best of both worlds.

15

Even the Ocean Has a Shore

I went through a period in my life when I was a bit suspicious of happy Christians. I mean the kind who bounced through life insisting that no Christian had any right to be *un*happy—ever. I remember one, in particular, who seemed to be in a state of perpetual motion, hopping up and down and wiggling her fingers and exclaiming, "Joy, joy, joy." She never sat still, and she never stopped talking. I secretly named her Miss Silly Putty. "She dresses like an ice-cream cone," I would mutter to myself. She was the type who (as Betty Pershing once said) would ring your doorbell and twitter, "I just ran over your dog."

I was at a stage in my life where it seemed most proper and appropriate to be dour. I didn't mind joy, if it was accompanied by a beatific smile, with a trace of sadness underneath, indicating great spirituality—and if it was expressed in religious homilies, so much the better.

At that time I was under the influence of a group of Christians who knew every gloomy bromide in the book.

"It is no wonder that Christians are so sad," they would mourn. "Look at what a state the world is in."

And I would agree.

I even stopped listening to my radio during that period, for it would only confirm what we already knew. There was nothing to be happy about; there was no humor in anything.

But genes will out, and environment, too.

It took awhile for my transformation, but it was inevitable. All my happy genes and all my upbringing came slowly to the top and pushed up and out, like frozen cream on the old milk bottles that got left on the porch on a winter day. It finally became apparent that I could not remain in this austere company any longer; I was a heretic. I was at the end of a long, long line of happy people.

Of course, they had no right to be happy, but somehow they never got hold of this fact. If their happiness depended on "happenings," they, of all creatures, would have been most miserable, for the saga of my family was tragic. I won't go into it here; you'll just have to take my word for it. It is a history of untimely deaths, tragic misadventures in business, losses of money, alcoholism, and a vast assortment of miscellaneous mishaps. Why they were happy I shall never know, except that a happiness strain seemed to go down through the family, from generation to generation.

I did not know this for many years. I did not observe it, until I saw it in my own mother.

She was a happy woman.

To sum up one's mother by simply saying she was a happy woman is ridiculous. It becomes significant only because, from a human standpoint, she had very little to be happy about. She lost my father in World War I (I was three months old) and struggled from there on—all downhill.

She supported my sister and myself—and my grandmother, and three other children who were orphans and products of broken marriages. The vicissitudes and vagaries of our growing up I'll not describe here; they're all in *There I Stood In All My Splendor.* I think the main point here is that she always told us we were *blest.* We were encompassed and surrounded by God Himself. Why should we not be happy? She was determined—not by preaching, but by her pragmatic approach to the Christian life—that we would never be otherwise. Thus she was, and thus she remained, throughout my childhood and beyond.

Years, many years later, I left my two small sons with a baby-sitter and stayed at her home nights, to take care of my stepfather, whom she had married after we were grown.

He was dying of cancer. I slept on a couch in a room adjacent to his, so I could hear him in the night.

One night I was awakened by a groan from his bedroom, and I sprang from my couch to go to him—but Mother had already leaped from her bed in another room, and we collided in the dark by a rocking chair, where she smashed her instep into the sharp point of a rocker. She lifted her foot and groaned with pain. It was the kind of pain that made you see stars.

"Oh, Mother, Mother," I wailed, "I'm so sorry." I put my arms around her, only to find that she was *laughing*.

"It's all right," she said. "It's nothing that won't be okay in a week or ten days. I'll just take an aspirin and call you in the morning." And we clung to each other, laughing hysterically for a moment, before I flew—and she hopped—to his bedside to attend to his needs.

Were we without feeling? I think not. We were both totally exhausted, for one thing, and laughter is very close to tears.

I didn't think about it then, but I'm thinking about it now. Why? Why her inexhaustible sense of humor? Why did it bubble up like that, and where did it come from?

I don't know; it was just there. And if you think of that as "flip," I might mention that at that stage of her life, mother was blind.

I rest my case.

So it goes on.

"She's too flip," I overheard while I was coming out of an auditorium after speaking.

"I thought she was never going to get serious," another said. "But she did, finally."

"Oh, but up until that time, she was flip—too flip—*very* flip."

It was on the third *flip* that I realized they were talking about me.

I glanced briefly at their faces.

Shades of the ghosts of yesteryear!

They looked suspiciously like the Christians of my "dour tour" through Gloomsville, those many long years ago.

For some perverse reason, I was gratified by their remarks. There had been low points in my life when I'd feared that the strain of joy and optimism in my forebears might have petered out, and that my mother might have gotten the last of it. If *they* thought I was flip, then all was not lost.

I forgave them on the spot.

"Oh, Miss Silly Putty, wherever you are," I moaned in my soul, "forgive me. I never should have judged you. How could I have possibly known whether or not you were shallow? And how could I have presumed to fathom your depth?"

I guess Oswald Chambers said it best:

Beware of allowing yourself to think that the shallow concerns of life are not ordained of God; they are as much of God as the profound. It is not your devotion to God that makes you refuse to be shallow, but your wish to impress people with the fact that you are not shallow, which is a sure sign that you are a spiritual prig. Be careful of the production of contempt in yourself, it always comes along this line, and causes you to go about as a walking rebuke to other people because they are more shallow than you are. Beware of posing as a profound person; God became a baby.

To be shallow is not a sign of being wicked, nor is shallowness a sign that there are no deeps; the ocean has a shore. The shallow amenities of life, eating and drinking and talking and laughing are all ordained by God. These are the things in which Our Lord lived. He lived in them as the Son of God, and He said that "the disciple is not above his Master."

Our safeguard is in the shallow things. We have to live the surface common-sense life in a common-sense way; when the deeper things come, God gives them to us apart from the shallow concerns. Never show the deeps to anyone but God. We are so abominably serious, so desperately interested in our own characters, that we refuse to behave like Christians in the shallow concerns of life.

Determinedly take no one seriously but God, and the first person you find you have to leave severely alone as being the greatest fraud you have ever known, is yourself.

I know this now. I have learned to look at everyone, including myself, with compassion, and not without some humor.

I don't know where you are coming from, dear reader, but I think, in many cases, I have been there, too. I have known rejection, desertion, betrayal, and despair. And yes, I have inflicted pain on others, too often (once is too often). And yes, I have lusted after a man in my heart, and yes, I have feet of clay.

But I still believe in laughter, for "A merry heart doeth good, like medicine."

I didn't say it.

God said it.

I've grown wiser, I hope, now that the muscles in my arms are hanging down on the wrong side.